Engenderings

Cairns Clery

chipmunkapublishing
the mental health publisher

Published by
Chipmunkapublishing
PO Box 6872
Brentwood
Essex CM13 1ZT
United Kingdom

http://www.chipmunkapublishing.com

Copyright © Cairns Clery 2012

ISBN 978-1-84991-719-3

Chipmunkapublishing gratefully acknowledge the support of Arts Council England.

Acknowledgements.

With special thanks to Liz Graham, without whom 'Searching for a Home' would never have been achieved. Also to Jane Saotome for her continuous poetic dialectic with me. To all my dear friends, including Margaret, Penny, Ann and Bob, Jackie, Christine and John and many others who know who they are. Thank you. To my children for putting up with me and to Bridget for not giving up on me - I am so grateful.

Engenderings

Contents

Engenderings

Paradise Left.

Perfectly composed, though naked, Eve was quick as silver,
Well within herself, not neurotic at all in discreetly discovering
The magic charm of secretly cheating in an Eden as warm
As her aching womb. And as it was the Creator she was conning
It somehow felt especially neat. With an innocent, sidelong look
She squeezed her hands between her knees to stop herself from
Being seen about to taste the oddly sharpened circularities
Of the apple. Hiding behind appreciative sighs of semi-genuine
Admiration for the anodyne works of her maker, her true soul
Desire was to bite hungrily on the fruit of the knowledge-tree.
With mock indignation she protested she wasn't wanton to the
Wicked and tiny androgynous serpent now curled sleepily
In her lap dreaming of difference, making sure her Progenitor
Heard her. That He was deaf to her lie was a blinding truth and
She exulted as He and Adam discussed the meaning of Necessary.
The time was now ripe for swiftly cramming apple after illicit
Apple into a tummy whose emptiness mirrored the eternal life
She was so sick of. And which felt like a tomb. As the green
Juices ran she wanted above all to be free to go to fucking hell
If need be; to live eternal life through death and procreativity.
She longed for blood and children to give her feelings succour.
The snake in her lap stirred and whispered the word 'Mother'
And she felt no deep sense of belonging or identity at all with
All the prettiness surrounding her, recognising only the darkest
Space between the stars above as hers. So she ate the worm as
Well, swallowing it whole. Her stomach heaved. And lurched; but
Her dinner stayed down and she didn't mention what she'd done as
Adam droned on about Choice versus Responsibility. Ignoring him,
She said whether or not he came with her she was leaving right now
Because she wanted to step out into uncertainty, old age and cold.
Maybe she'd discover how to cover herself with colourful clothes
Or feathers, or sleep with wild and dangerous animals. Whatever;
She would die, but this wasn't living. Adam, all talk till then, lit up
With life of his own. Thus enguiled they left; their genitalia fanged
And dripping. Meanwhile, pristine, still, Eden is still now forever a
Glorious golden garden which always was, yet still never has been.

Meaning

It is always there in what I just miss.
And in what I cannot actually describe;
In the irony of writing all this
Knowing I won't surpass mere diatribe;
And in intuitive understanding
Of where I am trying to take you with my words.
It is always just beyond me, and in
Everything not present. It is absurd
That so many people seem to seek it
As if actually we were not how we are
(Programmed to yearn but never to reach it).
As if we really did evolve from the stars.
It's as if 'as if' was not 'as if' at all,
That yearning and seeking themselves are the goal

DOG MOPE *

I am dimly aware
Of how little
I see beyond

Intimations
Which illuminate
Piercingly
And are gone
As soon as they are seen

As ephemeral
As I am
As real
As me
For a moment

Residuating glimmers blaze
Gold and grand and shining
- So what? -
So when
I turn to them
And gaze

Their
Absence
Is absolute
And blinding.

*Although 'Dog Mope' is obviously an anagram of 'God Poem', I wrote this when both my father and his black Labrador dog, 'Taxi', were still alive. Like my father, Taxi would often sit looking very puzzled, as if he was willing to be aware of his limitations if he could be. This vision/these words are from his point of view.

Pain's **NOT** punishment and you're **NOT** guilty

Pain's meaning is so easily religiosified;
Supremely prominent, powerful
And so easily suffered,
Pain is the perfect panacea for self-importance.
It is the autocratic avatar of all our endings,
Regal in the unquestionable absoluteness of its existence.

Like liquid electricity
It washes into every crevice, finds each sensitive spot
With serene alacrity,
Flooding it faster than the speed of light
As it bathes in its own autonomy and basks,
Flashing with its own bitter-sweet victoriousness to enlighten you.

Then it can sit stagnant, sluggish at best,
As its searing yet desultory pulses stop pleasure in everything,
Even the small things, like feeling snug with the honeybees
Humming and golden as they slip between the last petals of summer
In the late blue sunshine, oblivious to the electric waters
On whose face they flit.

Pain's Pyrrhic enjoyment in precisely being able to find
The right neural pathways to make its presence felt,
Is in no way spoiled by being poised, shockingly,
Between the beginning and end of its own passing.
Pain is the sometimes not so stealthy king of the dark angels who deep-knows
That he's purposed to draw your attention to the present. Here. Now.

The absolute imposition of Pain's imperial certainty is so real
You could draw as many breaths as you wished and more
Before he drowned you or stopped your heart. He is always and eternally
Grateful for your suffering, knows that so long
As he evokes your feelings and attention to knowing
That now is forever, he is doing his job

And is completely content for you to know too
That he brooks not the slightest opposition.
So you can also understand that it is your very vitality
He is expressing. Your very own!
He is the spirit of light and water, of seeing and feeling,
And the corona of your cries is his crown.

Realising this can make Pain's waters recede
Can cause this wicked winged king to fly,
And, if you wish, to take you away with him into the void,
Darker than darkness where you are free to be no more.
Or, he can leave you here naked and trembling, awash
With light-left-behind, full of the emptiedness of release.

Meanwhile the bees and the flowers, the hugs and the kisses
Can carry on as if there is no tomorrow, no once and future
Agonising current of charged particles mass-stabbing all their cells.
No, each and every one can enjoy taking care to trip gratefully
Or scent colourfully through each and every given moment in the wondrous
Adventure of the everyday. They can simply be. Now.

LEAF SHEAVES

Strange the way every day configures themes to dream on other nights;
each stray glance or chance remark is gathered and togethered
with serene indifference and no deference whatsoever to decorum.

And is grafted, miraculous and matter-of-fact, to the amalgam tree
rooting and branching from gene-pool to black hole, validating
absolutely every last leaf of thought and feeling, giving it matter,

giving it meaning.... In the dark departure lounge of deepest sleep,
therefore, where even the ghosts have ghosts, even there, where
the whisperings of atoms tell of the terrifying and sexual

connectedness of everything, images and words unfurl
in dizzied proliferation, knitting narratives from every last straw
sym-binding and baling them into possibility or experience,

out of silence.... I see now forever being born in the lives of all
of us and all the ancestors and all the descendants of all
of us, all always knowing this is how it is and has to be.

Worm

I don't know how to feel.
I am always 'after the event'.
Hindsight hurts, makes me feel stupid.
Foresight, farsight, insight is in others.
I spend my life trying to get it right,
In other words: I always get it wrong.
I think well, I speak well, but my feelings
Are beyond me. I am frightened they come
Completely naturally to others and that therefore
I will always be one to wriggle in the dark.
I am telling you so now
In this quasi-poetic form for fear of crying.

Lulla bye

Batten down now,
Nice and snug.
Bid your life good day now
Give yourself a hug.
Who knows what tomorrow may bring?

Porch

I don't know whether I'm coming or going.
Being here, betwixt and between, feels like home.
I can belong in and out at one and the same time.

It may be miraculous, a traversing of life and death.
Or I'm a ghost, neither who I was nor who I will be.
I don't know, and not knowing feels like home.

So I doss de-sexed beneath my blankets, disembodied.
Then I look both ways and am resexed, reembodied:
Someone who belongs everywhere and doesn't exist.

Touched by the impossible marriage of opposites
I am determined to take no sides or both sides.
And remain stuck at the door, a stone changeling.

PORCH TOO

Ready for departure, destination unknown.
Driven organically, the last goodbye.

Finally all breaths can be allowed out
To play. No more schooling inhalations;

The point of it all was always simply
To cease, whether in rage or at peace

Was immaterial. The end could be heard
When the first infant cry was sounded.

Now being borne into helpless expiry
Time, passaged and uniqued, is wrapped,

A free complimentary gift to take away
As the comforting darkness descends.

WORDSHIPPING ANIMALS

I am too aware of how nothing beyond the birth
And death gates to these golden fields of skin
And feeling is available. The problem is

There is so much more than I can imagine
That I can never know except in dreams
And mapful glimpses of faraway stars.

Nothing can compensate for the awful
Absence of all real knowing. And all of life is
Always about trying to find more of

The devilish little details which together
Might pan-define the shape and shine
Of the encrypted structure holding it all together.

Speaking as a god it is humiliating,
But as a wordless animal it is accepting it that can come
Too easily. To be human is to be halfway

Between, per-longing for omniscience in the
Belly of the beast, whilst delicately making and
Mapping the clearest of tracks.

Succumbing

seeking succour,
like atavistic slumber,
is an easy slide
back into blind
animaling ingestion -
eyelids bald, mind shut

the mothered
dreaming infant head
envelops the world,
as invisible as air,
viewing all
seeing nothing;

and yet the scent
of the breast being
nuzzled bears
a curious relation
to the obscured
sénse of self

as if inner and outer
were interchangeably
connected, perspectively
identical – the mind
being touchable,
the body ether.

the mother a child
whose solemnity
is a game of fuck-you
baby for casting me
in the role of primitive,
why should I love you?

and her neat jealous
rage breaks the
callow ignorance
cherubing her child
prompting it to bite
and bawl oblivious

to her honesty.
then she angrily
swallows acceptance,
seduced and beguiled
by minute reflections
from her mother-child

into finding herself.
infantalised she dozes,
enveloping the whole
world, seeing everything,
and each silent breath
drawing in dreams.

Gilted guilt bath.

Defeated and stinking,
The emperor's old clothes
Go in the warm wash cycle.

At the flick of the switch
From actual responsibility
To ersatz innocence

They ruminate around what
Was and might have been,
Churning in a detergent

Of throwaway excuses
And anxious empty lies.
Then rinsed and spun

In dizzy ordinariness
They're tumble dried
And dropped,

Forgotten on the floor
For future ironing.
As obsolete as history.

ANTS

As light as air, yet displacing space, I can't believe we exist.
And don't talk to me about logic: madness marches here.

Obsessed by Purpose, there is no point to anything else.
When anything else intrudes – which is most of the time –

I am listless depressed, longing to be powdered or squashed,
Incapable of any kind of indivisibility or acceptance,

Just doing doing doing, in lines as straight as dyes even
As I go round in circles go round in circles go round

Organised from without by some sick sense within of order
In uniformity. The trend I follow is set by decree.

I even believe that I am the author of my own destiny
And there is no question that I know precisely what to do.

Snaked

Pssst!…You sshould know
I glow nuclearly
With knowing
All iss well
When I'm kindnessssing –
I feel I belong,
My warmth being wanted
And returned with interessst,
Tho my secret skinlessness
Grins with abject despair,
Ducking and weaving
Behind my friendly face,
Like some awful playground
Ghoul ssseeking sssome acccceptance,
It's actually ssssoothed, re-balmed
By interactional effectiveness, social sssskill,
Into fine upssstanding conventionality –
Zippedy doodah'd then hidden away
With a veneer so polisshed and rayed
That everyone can ssee themselves in me
Whenever the fancccy takes them
Without knowing a thing about it.
Sssneer at my motivation if you will,
Regard me with disgust or disdain
But we are of the ssame kind,
You and I, and all of uss,
So I will do it to you too
When the meaning of my words
Merges with everything elssse
Which, like your earliest years
You will have alwayss forgotten.
And when I do, deja-vu will warm you
To me and you will smile and we will play,
Pulsing kindness mutually like ssuns,
As if I wasn't what I am, and nor were you.
And neither of us, changelings, will know
Excccept intuitively that we tasste
Oursssselves and each other with
Forked tongues and need the driesst
Of dessserts for such dissembling to thrive.
Anxiousssly looking behind us, alwayss checking,
I fear we won't know we are genuine any more,
Or that insignificant, legless, neurotic though we are
Our authenticccity may well
Truly be remarkable

Cameled

The long arrythmic caravanning across this dreary vastness
Takes it out of me more than You realise, Esteemed Driver,
With Your divine purposefulness always the overriding
Priority. I am imagining that I can pass through the eyes
Of needles, that my awkward rolling gait and literally lumpen
Body can be transformed into something altogether different,
That death is more than the wind-sucked reduction to dust
It appears to be, and that this trekking finally gets us home.

As You can doubtless appreciate I am clearly going quite mad,
Mirage-shimmer shaking the foundations of my conciousness
And giving me ur-reason to hope that the impossible exists
With the same finite tangibility as this parched scrolling desert.
Would You recognise me if I changed? Would who I am merge
With who I was and who I will be? Would You be disconcerted
And dismount? What then? Would I come back to my senses
And be glad to be the misshapen product of my parents loins?

All things considered I think I would rather You showed me
No mercy. Please apply Your whip hand without compunction.
I see the city of dreams ahead is peopled with the flesh and blood
Experiences of all creatures great and small, and I would enter
It without fear to join them. When these words are all that's
Left of my track across the hot dry waste, when I am gone,
We will all be there drinking together from the same fountain,
Discussing our different journeys as if there were no tomorrow.

THE OSTRICH POSTURE

I want to make sense of all this,
Attach meaning to shape, depth and relationship,
Find the purpose to what happens
So that the sweet solace of
Knowing-What-It-Is-All-About
Can be my secret garden, small and walled,
But stocked with exotic plumaged
Paramours, perfect dreams, passion fruit
And peach, and over which I can preside
With an important, leggy strut,
Striding with genuine pride,
That inside I am safe from all predators.

Sans my usual anxious,
Spurious detachment from all I survey,
My face, glum as prunes, naturally
Will never show what I know
Or reveal what I feel;
Mouth fashionably pursed, I will trill
With sophisticated badinage
Leaving a pearletted faecal trail
Of sarcasm and irony
Just like any other lanky
Memory-crashed careerer
With long legs and a large feathered bum.

Because it would not be right to parade
My certainty like some fascist
Concerned to offer pity but no commitment
To the lost and unsure.
And anyway how would I know
I wasn't just deluding myself,
Confusing knowledge with belief
And being so stuck up
That I dared not risk
Ever being found out?
Now, would you please excuse me
I must search in this sand for grubs!

Albatross

Once, I crossed the undulating grey
Storm-tossed oceans only to find my
Hatchling dead in the shell of her egg.
It wasn't my grief, but the feeling
Fuelling it which Creation and
Destruction sought. I cried aloud
In the teeth of the gale, and the colours ran
Beautiful, unbearable, borealised –
From my heart. Which is how I know

Every time, processionally,
A slow wide wheel winds
Through the vast mind's sky,
Orbiting who I am
In a grand solo flight
Which panoramas why
I had to be this way,
I cry, as if the only one,
'Why me?' Every time.

And in reply the detail sings
Through flume from waves piled
Life on lifetimes high,
That luck has made it thus for everyone
And your self is as unique
As your experiences are not.
It spans continents and bridges time
As precisely as these words
Seek out your understanding.

So hear them, yellow-beaked, ungainly
Though they are when grounded,
In flight they will carry you beyond
These unnavigable starless seas
To the breath in your breast.
And though you will often bleed
And will certainly die, you must know
Who you are and what you have felt
Gives this globe its meaning.

Untitled

I don't want to say
I think I'm going mad
I'd prefer to talk about overloaded circuits –
Be a machine and simply cease functioning –
Or about cracking up –
Be a wall and just crumble.
What I cannot take is
Every passing thought
As an assault on my feelings,
Every perception
A prompt to cry.
It makes me want
To infantilise myself
And nipple-ate you,
Close my eyes
Wish I was dead
And drift into the dreamscape
Where transformation is absolute.

In the dream
My curled eyes are made of glass,
The sun is oiled and
I can live with who I am.
Madness, like sadness
Is just another state
And I matter to myself
No more or less
Than I do to you.
The comfort is
That I can be anything
I want, which lets me
Want to be me.
There is though
No waking from it:
Once the threshold is crossed
Sanity is sanitised, be-ringed, because
In the dream there is no dreaming.

MONKEY

Whenever I look
In the mirror for my face
I cannot find it.

Instead monsters lurk
Intimately strange,
Unnervingly familiar,

And glib in the glass,
Playing pantomime parts
With cheesy chimpanzee grins.

And they dine on my scrutiny
With a cannibal grace though
They're very scared to be me.

So I seek solace in denial –
Cos I'm hurt and ashamed
And I spit: neither can you be me.

At that they tremble then freeze,
Stone-statued they bleed,
But smiling still glad they're not me.

Which sears my sight
With the truth that lies:
It's easier to look than to see.

DAMNIMAL

I COME FROM BEYOND
THE GATES OF ARRIVAL AND DEPARTURE,
WHERE DARKNESS AND LIGHT
ARE BLINDINGLY UNSHADOWED,
TO FIND MYSELF HERE
WITH A FACE
LOOKING OUT ON THE PROCESSION
OF ACCIDENTS AND INTENTIONS
SHAPING HOW I HAVE TO BE.
ONLY THE GOLDEN FLOW
OF THE SUBTERRANEAN
DREAM STREAM
KEEPS ME CONNECTED
FROM GATE TO GATE.
I WOULD THAT I COULD SWIM IN IT.
INSTEAD IT WASHES UNDER AND OVER ME
WHILE I'M SLEEPING LIKE A STONE
IRRADIATING MY BLOOD
WITH A SOFT SEDUCTIVE GLOW
OF MEANING AND PURPOSE;
RENDERING REDUNDANT
MY MYOPIC ATTACHMENT
TO ALL MY DIFFERENT DAYTIME NOISES.
THE ROARINGS AND BLEATINGS
THE CAWINGS AND SHRIEKINGS
THE MOOS AND COOS
WILL ONLY SOUND TRUE
IF I CAN LET THEM GO.
I KNOW.
TO CLING TO THEM
IS TO ACT AS IF
THERE ARE NO GATES,
NOR SLUICING THROUGH THEM
THE DREAM STREAM
RUNNING AS A RIVER
TO AND FROM THE SEA BEYOND.
BUT I CAN'T HELP IT.

Moled, but ringing bells anyway

Fortunately I always fail
To actually see the future
Even though I can read it
In my memory of stars.
I can tell you, for instance,
That everything you fear
Will come to pass
Will indeed do so
But come the final
Dew-dropped dawn
It won't matter any more.
Not as pain anyway.
Furthermore I know that you are
Always full of transferences
Exquisitely arc-angled to the nth degree,
With which you tamper and toy,
Transform, re-transfer or destroy
In an avant-glorious profusion
Of self-unfolding and defining
The like of which my dark stupidity
Can't begin to imagine down here.
(DINGDINGDING! Its <u>YOU</u> I'm speaking to).
Which was what we came here for.
Wasn't it? Or wasn't it?
I have no eyes. I cannot see.
And anyway I have no one to do it with
(DING) Transferencing, I mean,
Except in my dreams,
And I dream I do it with you.
And even if I don't
I do not care, I tell myself,
It does not matter
Cause I can dark-dig
Deeper than the roots of any tree
In all those outsight worlds of yours.
So I dream that though
I am deep-dark-digging
Down here, alone and unable to speak,
I have magic! I am a secret
Underground campanologist
And my bells ring to tell you
Hush-now-everything-*will*-be-alright.
And my dream has the power
To take itself to you
Embracing your anxiety with words
Whose dissonant **(bong)** can
Nevertheless warm you
With the sweet sound of surrendering

If you want. But courage is required.
Experiences will shape you.
Your sense of who you are
Will be as plastic as the
Limbic flexibility of a contortionist.
Your openness may shut out
The full horror behind mortality's
Bland universal mask.
(DINGDINGDONGDONG)
I mean death, which alone is shared
Even though it separates us.
But if you are able to accept it
You somehow show it up
For what it is – a divine device
For concentrating our minds
On what matters: Love.
Acceptance. More love.
Things like that. Me and
You, my real but imagined friend,
With your feet planted firmly
On the ground I'm so busy under.
The ignominy, the shame
That such a device is necessary
Must mean that there is so much
(DINGDONGDING)
More to be done with all the
Arc-angeled transferences
In all their shocking fineries
And all their nth degrees.
Realising this you will want to despair.
But please don't. I need you.
If you give up, or go mad,
There will be no rhyme or reason
For me to root down here for you.
And I will surface to find
That all along you were as deaf
As I am blind.
I could not bear that too easily.
From my eyelessness
Tears would flow.
But I would not ask myself, even so,
Why I tried to console you
With the grubby findings
From my search below.
I would know from my memory of stars
You always meant so much to me.
(DONGDONGDONG)
You know, you know. You know.

The fake drake/duck fuck

All is swell
And duck sighs,
Dripping sticky
Drops from eggs
Whetted
Into stirring

Sloughed out
Suddenly or slow
Dick droops
Smiling
Still full
But soft, sated.

Such is the stuff
Of life vitally
Repatterning
Its own contradiction
Across time
Space and species

But the unifying dream,
Timeless and insubstantial,
Shapes itself through me;
Shaking
My integrity
Till it screams.

Anaconda

The deathstuary-seeking flow of
The dream is churning
Surging, brown and muddied
Angry with ignorance's ancient guilt
And cross-currented with
Amazon-like awarelessness
Of its own power –

A secret gene-stream has swollen and
River'd. I am riven by hysteria
Unintentionally shored by rigid
Trammeled Packages of Reason
Lined up in anxious serried banks of
Desparate sandbaggery
And purple purposefulness.

It would break free
And deluge who I think myself to be
With the fleshy silted fragments
Of a dredged up identity
Which I dutifully manicled
And weighted with the heaviest cairns
More than an eternity ago

It wants to dissolve who I am
To drown with all the others
We must merge with when we die.
So that whose distress is crying out
For help can again become a mystery
The solution to which, whoever it is,
Can only be found by how you see me.

So please see me as you want me.
Though I am naked and even as I shake
You unchain me and give me a shape
With your sightfulness. So you can smile
Whether I stay or gracefully glide away
Across the water, leaving a gentle swirl
For your feelings to wist for, your memory to trace.

PERCH

Temporal lobes pounding:
Pretending to be real.
Really pretending
And realising pretence
So successfully
That, well,
You wouldn't really know
Who I am. Not him.
Nor her. Nor how,
Secretly shafted,
I can still delight
In mingling so freely,
Smiling serenely in
Assent or demur
Repeatedly as required
And oiling, essentially,
Everyone's expectations
With perfectly gendered
Aptness and polite respect
Via the most fragrant
And fabulous of frontages.

Except, just maybe,
You can scent
The foetid smell of fear
Wafting from the folds
In the anguished flesh
Of my skinless soul,
Lurking softly below,
Lingering beneath the lining
Of my colourless coat
And shaping, sweetly, into a ghost
Which I must kiss
And suck back in
Like a dick or a tit
Whose embittered barb
Will pull off my lip
Unless it hooks me.
The fear is being seen
Naked in the dream stream
Swimming stupidly against the flow
As if I was mad
And didn't really know.

Cowed

Know now how
Brow-beaten
I've become by you.
I'm not going to grass
But I can no longer cope
With watching over you
With tremulous grazing
Anxiety, or swaying
Predictably towards you.
Lumbering heavily
Across fields of feeling
To nurture your manhood
With my deep understanding
Is breaking my back.
I cannot stand by anymore
Dark-eyed and staring
At your difference, unaware
Of what I don't understand
But feeling it like blood
Sluicing from the slice
I now would like in my neck.
I shudder to think
That I ached to make
You my master
And let you drink
My milk to stop me moaning.
I am outraged. And so tired.
Let my breasts burst
For I cannot be
What I'm not anymore
For you.
Nor can I be what I am
Without you
I must die.

COWED II

Let me go. I won't go far. I'll chew the cud.
I'll stand in mud. I'll look at you. And moan.
You can hurt me if you want before I go.
The shit is running down my legs so shamefully.
But at least I'm losing weight I suppose.

Look at your clothes. I can't believe I ironed them
Last week before your bovination of me set in.
I felt so content then that you'd given me a role.
I wanted to cry with happiness and welcomed
The way you would poke me with your desire.

It made me feel I was your secret truth, a sacred
Cow you could worship and adore knowing,
And you did know, I would do anything for you.
If I was always frightened of your lurid rages
I loved you for coming to me passionately afterwards

Pinning me down with your shining perceptions,
Clowning your apologies and genuinely making me
Smile (just) when I'd decided that only doing the dishes
Or hoovering the front room would prevent me
From breaking down like a child before you.

But I would cry later when we'd gone out together
And you were talking about yourself again.
But you didn't know. I don't know why but
I couldn't let it show. It would have been pornographic
Somehow, like deliberately appearing in a peepshow.

I wanted you to love me for myself. Not for what
I meant to you or how I looked. But you couldn't see
Past my eyes. And most of all I just wanted you
To be free to be yourself with me. Whoever that was
And whatever you did. You could use me as you wished.

And I wished you would, but you didn't. It was as if
By giving myself to you completely I became completely
Invisible. As if I wasn't really being me. The irony
Wasn't lost on you either but you didn't really care at all
And I recognised then that I was all alone.

But that is a fate far worse than wilful transformation
Into someone different, someone as selfish and moody
As you. I shrieked and sulked again and again until I didn't
Know myself anymore. Your initial alarm, which was pleasing,
Turned to bored derision. I realised I was your pantomime

And you were using me again to find out how you felt.
Even as you pitied me. And I let you patronise me
As I contemplated cutting myself, quietly, privately,
A little red gush all of my own. Not nature's, nor your's.
Just mine. A silent blood-song to and from myself.

Which was when it hit me that I was doing all this for you.
Or at least for both of us. I don't know where you end
And I begin but I do know now that when I offered myself to you
You were not interested because you knew I was already yours.
And you didn't even tell me. Please let me go. I'll moo for you.

Stranger in a Church

A stoned arched darkness, inscented and curving
Down like the God-mother's underskirt all around;
Allows the engendering imagination to soar up
And dream that the shadowy caping safety cache
Of the nave enables intercourse with the absolute.

The clean-pated old priest below proclaims his sinfulness.
Not aware that he is lying, his bespectacled chastity
And monotheistic ardour have genuinely averted any
Catastrophe of choice. As a believer he 'can address
The problem of evil', faithfully declare it to be a mystery,

And feel 'joy wit Jaysus. Death is the gateway to life', he
Says, solemnly kindling a candled celebration of mortality
Whilst inviting the thought of a hereafter. One or two
Congregational brows furrow in unison, snatching furtive
Upward glances at the idea of a divine birth canal.

But the rest remain cushioned on the breasts of certainty,
Heads respectfully bowed, wearing their Sunday best and
Humbly seeking spiritual succour without bitterness or regret.
We are all the many-who-are-called but here they are all
The few-who-are-chosen. And I feel like a spy with no side

With my redundant resentment of the human condition, and my
Neurotic self-absorption. So loneliness makes me look up, but
The architecture above is too sensual and too maternal and respect
Forces me to avert my gaze and look at the life within. Later I
Dream of a moving collectivity of lighted candles floating in the air.

Contrasexual.

Uncovering her secret receptivity, and resting irradiate on
The experience of being entered; without demur, simply giving
Taking, knowing all along this was what she'd wanted, she glistens

With temporarily being what he seeks, choosing to surrender
To his insistence. Her own needs widening and moved into pulling
Him in deeper. No point now in not being in for pennies and pounds.

But loosened into absolute enclosure she can not help screaming
For his soul as he slides out quietly and slips away, softened
By scoring into searching for his meaning somewhere else.

Had he not left like that, she might not have wanted him to stay.
But there is something rotten in the statement of a leaving
Like that which leaves her lusting not just to tear out his eyeballs,

But to become what she is not, nagging, forever dissatisfied and
Withholding hellishly. After all, she only asked to share his soul.
So she will prod him, the barer of her rod, until they feel the same.

And their marriage? Together they will ensure there will be no
Fit between their parts which is not mirrored by the parts
Which they fit between. They will deal death to *la difference.*

They will be anything they want to be, but always identically
Twinned by their need to trade tit for tat, like neurotic warlocks
Harlotting for the sake of it, simply because that is what they do.

Funereal (Crabbe Street, Aldeburgh 15/4/99)

Outside,
With time on its side
Waiting to come in whenever,
The elemental otherness of the heaved sea
Looms impossibly above the shingle, dark, luminous
And poised like pregnancy all along the quaint and fabulous shore.

Inside,
Puckered plucky strangers,
Strangely enfamilied and snappily dressed
Sip white wine and egg sandwiches, waiting for the
Service which will send the dead matriarch down into the dark
Hole which she'd always been in my father's head since she left him aged four.

A kindly
Enquiry from an unknown
Cousin who is as beautiful as dreams
About whether I have any others on my mother's side,
Elicits an unintended gattling unctiousness: only one, the other one died,
Shot his head off at Christmas time while his mother watched Morecombe and Wise.

She plunges
Dropping like a stone into
The sofa as she murmurs sympathetically,
Thinking of her own children and what else she hopes
They might be spared. Feeling like a ghoul and fearing that I will spear
Someone else's pure white soul if I say another word, I become silent and stare out to sea.

Half an hour later
In the pellucid watery light
Of the perfectly proportioned church
The fashionable young priest proclaims the emptiness
Of his grandchilded relationship with the deceased by telling all gathered
Here today about Harry, so like granny, who knew what he thought and whom he buried last week.

Her son, my father
Doesn't know why he's here,
But he learned long ago how to hurt so only
Looks out of place. My mini-skirted sister has brought him a basket
Of flowers to put by her grave. I prod him to pluck one and throw it on the coffin.
He does what he's told. Willingly, slowly going through motions he would mean if he could mean

In any April rain.
Then 'everyone is invited back
To the lighthouse for tea' and I imagine a real one flashing
Above them as they try to find comfort in shared memories of crockery
And white linened table-cloths fluttering like shrouds over all the situations like these
They'll ever have been to. Then the banked-up sea bursts, breaking over all of it, as if it didn't matter.

Aracnoid

Cupped and sagging
With the weight
Of water,
Sombre
September webs
Glisten
In the cold grey dawn.

And I,
Keening and numb,
Want to be as I am,
Alone
With the due
And the shocking
Electric stillness

Of spiders
Whose labours
Are purposed precisely
To externalise the pattern
And realise
The sticky dreams
Of the isolate

In an orgy
Of instantaneity
Designed to assuage
Hunger
And divert attention
Into the mindlessness
Of action and attack.

In the tranquil
Peace of the morning
The solip-savagery
Of sucking
And devouring
Requires no
Justification.

Statuesque

1.
Alone aged five or six
In the bright spring sun
Feeling faint
With a keening ache
Drawn from the dream stream
Felling me,
Leaving me prostrate
At the marble hem
Of the stylised madonna's
Shining stone skirts.

2.
Looking up and seeing
That transfiguring sun
Corona a halo round her head.
The whole world
Would be safe
Within her arms
If she wasn't alone with me.
I lay my cheek
On her warmed white feet
And cry.

3.
Though I know
She will be luminous
And life-saving
Through the darkened days
And numbed nights
Of my future life,
She is blinding now,
Absolute, unshadowed,
Beautifully searing my soul
With her comfort.

4.
Keeping my nose to the
Smooth polished rock
I desperately suck on her toes
And in return she conjures
The sun to switch our
Subtle substances
So that her stone
And my skin secretly
Become one flesh
And I am made hers forever.

5.
Unfrightened, made safe,
Who I am anymore
Becomes unclear
Though I know really
It does not matter
That I don't know
Whose toes now are my own.
I wipe my eyes.
I still can't stand
But everything is fine.

6.
Before he sent me out
The Cologned, clean priest
Had told me he knew
Who and what I really was
And what I must do
For him to show me
The Lamb of God.
He looked fierce when
I flinched at how fat
His fingers were

7.
But he told me it was
Alright: through him
I would be touched
By The Redeemer
And made good,
And to stay that way
I must be as silent
As the host
Inside the tabernacle.
I promised I understood.

8.
But I was hers, *pieta'd,*
Before I ever was his
And getting unsteadily up,
I watch the girlish procession
Wending its solemn
Summer-frocked way
Through the wisteria
To the infinite kiss
Of first holy
Communion.

9.
Standing now, I know
I will always be alone
With this, and I weep
For not belonging,
A changeling
Neither flesh nor stone
Nor ever one of us
Or one of them
However much I measure
The connections.

10.
I learn like you do
That I'll never find
Heaven without hell again
Nor truth without lies;
Which is all very well
But it is also too much
Too soon to find that
Belonging is both
To the stars and to the
Empty space between them.

mess-eye-annic

I need comfort
Lest I collapse
I need comfort
Because I'm boneless
All flesh and muck
I need comfort
Because my thoughts
Are lost in the world
I need comfort
Because my autistic
Heart is burning
With the acid blood
Of the isolate
I need comfort
Because I'm rudderless
And floating in fog
And my thumb
Has worn my teeth
To the roots
I need comfort
Because what was
Still is
And what will be
Is too
I need comfort
Because I cannot
Imagine anymore
What it is like
To feel safe
I need comfort
For the rivening
Role I've been given
Gives me nothing
And no-one
To align myself with
I need comfort
To accept who I am
To breathe to eat
And to sleep
I need comfort
For without it
My flesh will be
Consumed by fire
From the inside out
And I won't be able
To look after you
Anymore.
Please comfort me.

Dog's mope 2

I am breathing upon the face of the waters.
As you stare into the unfathomable depths.
It is my soft eyes that meekly seek you
And my teeth and claws which tear the veil
From the truth that I am there in everything
That you are and everything that you are not

I am breathing upon the face of the waters
I am the deaths and births bursting in and out
Of this world of words made flesh. I am the
Impossible, imaginable but unknown. I am
Your ovaries, your semen, and your gender.
I draw you together. And I split you apart.

I am breathing upon the face of the waters.
I am the sound of meaning and deafness to it.
The blast of the bomb, the motherless child.
I am the struggle, the hope and the despair.
Love me, hate me, or be indifferent,
I really don't care. Not unless you do.

I am breathing upon the face of the waters
And I need you more than that baby needs
Her mother. I need you to know who I am
When you see me, and to find me and
Adore me and look after me as if really
I was only lovable and wholly good.

I am breathing upon the face of the waters
Churning up the tides. Omniscient
I am the serenity of your reflection,
The undeceived directness of your stare,
The intelligence of your understanding
And the stupidity in pretending I'm not there

I am breathing upon the face of the waters
The palpitation in your heart is my fear of
Being found out: that though I am completely
Within and without you, your very insignificance
Renders me redundant; that and your choosing,
Despite it, still to love. You are my inspiration.

Queen of Korisa*

The beautiful egg-bearer's
Helpless tiny baby
With her sleepy
Mollassic suck
Never grew up
To be even
As milk-heavy
As her mother's breasts
Are now, slowly leaking
Her stalled lasting love
As she stares,
Bent-backed and broken
At the torched bodies
Of her child and her lover;
Tearing out her shaken hair
And wrapping it tenderly
Around their remains
Imagining that it crinkles
And cuddle-curls around
Them both and crackles
Into flames.
But it doesn't.
It simply blows away.
And her tears are dry
As out of the depths
She cries and cries,
Yearning to join them
In the dark comfort
Of All-This-Undone.
But like her teeth
Her mind is grinding,
Sharpening the edges
Of her grief into
A honed incandescence
Whose heat cuts
Into her reason.
And she wants to take them
Both back inside her again
By eating them bone
By burnt and blackened bone;
To have them be
With her forever.
After that she will pluck out
Her eyes and quietly wander
Out into the waste.

*A little town in Kosovo "mistakenly" bombed by Nato in 1999

Bleating the bleat

Maddened
By knowing
All this
Is in my own mind,
But knowing
That knowing
That
Makes no difference,
Is depressing.

Qamila

Now she has none to love or love her anymore she
No longer knows who she is exactly. Distracted
And anxious she follows scents around the house
Which she hopes will evoke how once she might have
Been when first she read *that* musty yellowed book or
Glued *this* pot back together again. But they only leave
Her with the immanence of her solitary life now.

Like a cairn laid waste across an abandoned road
Meandering through lost and fragmented dreams,
Her sense of her self is spread across the forgotten
Country which was her life when the silken scarves
She is now running her fingers through might have
Been worn for the shaping and colouring of her own
Feelings. If they'd been worn at all. Certainly

They were not for helping a sculptured old crow
Greedily scavenge over the entrails of memory
For scraps of what her mother was like then, or how
Her father always ignored her just when she needed
Him not to, or how jealously she guarded her journal
Before discarding it with her training shoes, aged fifteen,
For all the usual distractions of adult emptiness. She

Cannot remember now why it is so important to peck-
Peck at the past, nor whatever can be gleaned from it;
Just that she will never find herself again unless she
Does so, and the more she pecks the more her beak
Sharpens, her eyes bead and her voice roughly saws.
But it doesn't really matter when no-one can see her
Degradation, nor know that once she was wingless and

As beautiful as babies are. And the immanence of the now
Was a brave new world of opportunity not oppression.
She can feel like that again, of course, alone with her feathers
And her ticks, her calluses and claws, looking at her
Motivations and searching for their source. As long as
She's alone with it and no-one can see. She is sure she can.
But it must be in private so that no-one can see her at all.

There are only two ways of tying coloured silken scarves
To the knotted ankles of caustic crows and then watching
Them fly fearlessly over hedgeless downs into an unknowing
Clouded sky: by abstention – risking no human contact, living
In peerless analytic solitude like Qamila, or by daring to kiss
That which is different and embrace the present love brings,
Knowing that you will be left with all the hurt. Like Qamila.

forge

Hushed fear and restrained joy in equal measure echo perpetually down through the silent corridors of the hospice and the maternity ward alike. Guardians of the gates to and from the unknown, the quiet unharried staff have a respectful awareness of their importance and good fortune in being present at the transformational crux between nothing becoming everything and everyone no-one. All the time

the occasional random howl of the dying or newborn and the anxious choked sobs or happy
cries of relatives punctuate the eternal presence of such places with the human reality of just
how difficult it is leaving and entering time and space. It feels as if the gods themselves can't understand this, and need the process of becoming and unbecoming to be a struggle, just to know how real it is.

And I, I am aware of how damaged I am, how unbaked, half-baked and overdone to a cinder
I can be; how regardless of our individual personalities, the same seems more or less true for everyone, and I can't help thinking then that we are all an experiment, the gods' way of trying to find what love is, in being structured so that the finding of it falls between hope and experience, birth and death.

When I wonder why, all I can come up with is some dim notion that maybe it is our very vulnerability which makes us so important, (and we must be to be put through all this milling), our inability to fully understand, our moral frailty, our self-importance and conceits, and our capacity to be kind and to be gentle. Without birth and death to contain them, these disparate qualities would be quite meaningless.

That is what I tell myself: nothing would be learned without each of us individually knowing we will die.
But it doesn't make it any easier to bear of course. What makes it easier is knowing you; and knowing that we are only ever actually all alone at the moment of passing through the birth and death gates, and even then the experience is so absolute that while it lasts our human feelings can surely wait a while.

In the meantime, however isolated or sorry for myself I am, it always seems to be in relation
to you. I do not mean to be a burden to you by this, to make you feel that it is you who makes
me feel that way and therefore must differentiate more, if necessary fight, or even kill to be separate from one another. But at the same time I need you to know me, and I know our differences not our similarities connect us.

And so between the infinite perspective of archetypal absolutes and eternal truth, and the tiny apparently trivial minutiae of feelings unfolding in everyday relationships, there is literally a world of difference. But making the connections known between them matters to me nearly as much as you do. I cannot imagine that they are not to be found between us. I am certain that we cannot find them on our own

and that the gods who relied on us to do this work without realising that it is we who hold the candles, now can't exist without us. Whether we are figments of their dreams or they of ours, is immaterial. What really matters is that we all should know we need each other. Without the gods there will be no feeling of measure. Without us there will be no measure of feeling, nor need anymore for birth or death gates.

So let us play. Let's make what we can and what we must of all the situations and accidents
which happen across the lengths of our lives. During the years we have between the maternity ward and the hospice, (if we should be so lucky), let's breathe it all in avidly and evenly. Even the dark despair and the terrible pain which will afflict every one of us can be lived with if, despite it, we can still find love.

Anxietic

i
think
being
at
ease
with
myself
requires
me
to
recognise
i
never

will
be;
that
as
i
am
now
and
ever
shall
be –
(not
wanting

to
be
me),
is
how
whoever
i
am
wants
me
to
be
really.

am
i
all
alone
with
this
or
is
it
like
that
for
you?

CONTINUUM

Sometimes this me
is that me
and that this
and
neither really
feels like me at all.
Sometimes all the me's
are almost undeniably mine
and I think I know
concisely who I am.
At such times it genuinely
doesn't matter
one iota
that a later me will wince,
Or that an earlier one
would gladly
avoid all this.

Sometimes
unavoidably,
Not one of them
will do.
None
is any truer
to my self
than any other;
and I will not
place a bet
that who I am
and who I think
I think myself
to be
Can coincide
With all the will in the world
Except accidentally

The Lady in the Lake

For a secret
Miracle
To occur
On the dark floor
Of the amniote lake,
The statue knows
She must alter
Her structure;

Become
Porous as pumice,
Light
As air,

Unthread herself
From the sulphuric
Blanket
Suck-holding her
Down in the depths
Of the mire
And slowly float
Up

To the frightening sun
Which will warm her
And soften her
Into breathing
And feeling
Safe with being
Alive. Then

She must just
Trust
The hum
In the air,
And freed from
Being petrified,
Cry
Like all the rest

Of the women
And babies
Whoever
Will have been

Borne,
That all is well
With listening
And with hearing
Songs of emotion
And relatedness
On the face
Of the waters;

Even with singing
Them sometimes,
As simply another
One of many
And not,
Nor ever,
The only one.

feline memories of halloween

Who I am has claws raking my trembling insides raw with anxiety…
Then I'm familiar: dark, invisible, mewling in helpless grief
At the suicide of my mother self and at being left alone

And abandoned here on her broomstick in the teeth of her night,
Witchless, wordless and howling with a need from which
There will never be release now I am alone with her desire;

Madly flying nowhere through an empty enclosing absence of light.
But safe, somehow, all claws clinging to her broom; a small thing
Dangerously wanting to fall to let go to be with her again down below.

I close my eyes and remember being at one with her, playing
With her make-up brush as she swept cobwebs of abuse from her
Pretty tired cheeks and pretended with bad foundation to be fine

Powder would patina my needy fluffy fur and though I could be safe
With her sometimes I did not understand why really we both wanted
To cry. I would nuzzle her jumper. She'd smile and I'd purr

Into her beautiful if alopetia'd hair, cute, minute, fierce and kittening
Again; knowing I was insignificant but trying to be the perfect little
Diversion for her harrowing despair as, absently, she'd stroke me.

That is now the fantasy, the solacing memory, as I cling to the broom
I used to sit on as she swept, swept. swept our sweet home clean;
And when she saw me weeping too she'd simply say 'I love you'.

I just wanted to be there forever with her then. All the time. And
Afterwards we'd go out and do the shopping. Later still, when the wizard
Got home, he'd take off his hat, make me make him a whisky

And then sit on me buck naked before he fucked her like a rabbit
And cuffed me like it was all good fun. And we all had to laugh
Or he'd kick both of us because we lacked a sense of humour.

MIRROR CALL

Morbrant ripples
From the dream stream
Twist and slide
All my alter egos
Into momentary existence,
As they cling together,
Desperate and drowning,
A multiple-limbed monster
Washed over and out.

And into the estuary
Where the shallow
Breadth of Time's water
Is taken away
By the sucking vastness
Of space waving at me –
At my miniscule particularity
As if I mattered somehow!

My me's and he's and she's
Shout out loud
That whether we do
Or don't, our presence
In the depths of embodiment,
In space and time,
And sleep and wakefulness,
Absolutely requires
Suspension
Of religious disbelief
To be sustained.

We otherwise will fall,
Planet and all,
Like a ball
Plum
Into the profundity
Of puddles;
Clearer than mud
That there is no
More-Than-This.

And each beached
Dream self,
Splattered now
And separated,
Would truly wail
As their light
Lay dying.

HEAVY RAIN

The unnervingly physical
Pattern of plashes
Of rain on tarmac
Is telling
Like pain or breath
Of considerable presence,

Of elemental otherness
Obstacled by another
Elemental otherness;
Their epi-fit
An intimidating thunder
Of impersonal events.

Their momentousness
Daunts and minimises
My terrified self-importance.
Tenderly I try to keep it
Safe, cupping it with one hand
And covering it with the other

In an inane instinctive
Umbrella of protection.
As if we mattered.
Then I hear the message
In the metre of the patterning
Of the rain: we do. We really do

ENGINE DRIVER

Desparate for a
Destination unknown,
I'm trying to switch tracks.

Eyes rolling anxiously,
Breath spits
Tongue speaks
Lips shout
Out loud
For fear
That Your ears
Will be closed
Like the blind
In the ticket office
Window was.

Relatively,
(In Einstein's sense),
And in relation to You
I am a runaway train
Rhythmically and raucously
Going around the bend
In the unending tunnel
And careering off the rails;

Into the complete
Crash of absolute
Wordless silence,
Which like light
Is so fast
That it stills the soul
With an impact
Sufficiently profound
That *–ultra alia –*
Not even an echo
(Like this one)
Can sound.

Then, funnelled
Up to where You are,
Where voices
Like lost property
Can be recovered again
Personally,
I want to blame You.

But it's too late now
And what would be
The point?

mad made

the rising sun syrups sanity
down in dollops – dawn
dripping on to the globular
mental pearls of illness grey
clouding and cuddling
my colour-forsaken brain.

for i have been rushing round
in circles, meting out
body blows in lieu of mind,
till my startled eyes rolled,
retinas detached from reason
by left hooks and right feeling.

but ultimately the awful anxiety
and enmity i have with Understanding
has been shafted
by its terrible light, and i imagine
i finally know the long shadows
cast along the length of my days.

The Hag

The nape of her neck tingles all over with real and imagined anxieties and
She is very tense, orifically closed, hatches battened down tight, pursed up
Against all possible comers, from rapists to lovers. And all she knows now
Is that she will not speak at all, ever, about what she has seen and done, for
Fear of madly repeating patterns, already repeated often enough, yet again.

Behind her blotched menopausal skin, her red-inked eyes and lank grey hair
There lurks a knowledge of lines and tracks, every connection cogged along
The length of her life. And now she has the power to sell tickets and direct
You wherever you want to go, she won't, she can't be bothered, not for yet
Another near-despairing traveller whose demands can drive her to distraction.

'Fuck off'n go where you like, just don't bother me'. Her silent derision is
Louder than the transcontinental express I want her to let me have a seat on.
'You know perfectly well that all you have to do is be–' but then the piercing
Bleat of the whistle and the huge hydraulic hiss of the brakes being released
Distract me from her signals and anyway I have never understood semaphore.

All I want is a single fare home and I say so. She ignores me, not concentrating
Either on her tiny gleaming demon doll of a baby sitting on her taut-skinned
Round belly. I hit myself in case I'm dreaming – she's old enough to be a great
Grandmother but its true: she is suckling a baby and is ballooned in advanced
Pregnancy. Is this really a train station or an obstetric ward for the elderly?

Or, starkly, am I raving now, a lunatic? If she won't give me a ticket I'll steal
Her baby. I am that desperate and I understand how she feels. She is scared
Too – to ever speak again, yet at the same time she doesn't care at all whether
She lives or dies. But she's attached to her baby even as she pays no attention
To it, almost as if she is wearing it –her– like her favourite old grey jumper.

The doll-baby keeps changing size and looks at me with the eyes of someone who
Might have lived many times before. She is dressed in red and has vivid black hair.
Like her hag-mother, she doesn't care at all what anyone thinks of her as she plays
With her mother's protruding navel. Nipple-like, this still conducts nourishment
To the baby who, hewn from Californian Redwood, may be a thousand years old.

But my train is leaving soon and I don't care – I WILL not be left behind. I'll get
My ticket myself. I'll go into the ticket-office whether she lets me or not, and key
My destination into the machine. Myself. I yell this at the old witch who shakes her
Head, opens the door and shows me in with a small smile. Inside I lose all sense of
Who I am or where I am going. Enclosed by her rumbling darkness I am tunnelled

And trained…made small…and curling into a ball I suck my thumb, gestating,
Growing and developing into someone I do not recognise at all, the nape of my
Neck tingling with all the unspeakable real and imagined events that will befall me
When I have become an old witch and a grandmother, working at the station to
Feed my family, with no memory or sense of who I once was or where I was going.

amalgam

I have seen thousands of rainbows alight simultaneously on the woods.
And I have seen the sheering majesty of unclimbed mountain slopes.
I have also seen the neediness in your cheeks flush to be recognised.
And I've seen you bravely pretend not to be rebuffed by my balefulness.

I know I'm the object of your idealisations. The need to be seen for who
You are is so overwhelming that you cling on to your wondered image
Of me as if I really was as oh-so-perfect as you would like me to be. And
I am half withered, prematurely aged, by your wanton misperceptiveness.

How, in all truth and lies, can I ever live up to what you want me to be?
I just can't. But in not doing so, I let you down as much as if I did. I cry
Out simply to be seen for myself, just someone who has sometimes seen
Different things from you in a wide world requiring all sorts to make it.

Just as you do. It breaks our aching bones to be each other's carrier. I feel
Like I am full of prostheses bracing me ironically in the starving teeth of
Your unfulfilment. Because you are also chewing me up and consuming
Me, as if with me inside, you would somehow become who you really are.

But actually I cannot survive being eaten, and chunks of you are missing
Too, if I could but see it. The fact is I can no longer see you at all. Not at all,
Now that you have taken my eyes. We are anathema – you cannot move and
I am blind, although I find eyelessness and the inability to weep are not identical.

Neither of us know who we are anymore. Parts of me, I know, are simply
Indigestible. Parts of me would not be strong enough to carry myself alone
Even if they were still whole. But I am eating you too, even as you devour me.
We should stop now we are monstrous. Will you be my eyes? I'll be your legs.

You can find the way to the secret forest of rainbows hidden behind the high
Mountain walls of all our aches, errors and failings, and I will take us to it. Our
Inchoate body with its impossible doublings and its strange gaping absences
May well be discarded when we get there. Because we might just be in heaven.

low tide

goose-pimpled star-fish sometimes wish
that they could wallow in their rock-pools
incognito; that the ice-cold stillness of the
stones and sea-weed they share their bowls
with could be put in stasis, and the huge
chundering rush of the turned to in-coming
sea could be put on hold; allowing dreams to
range across the shore in impossible forms:
bloody, battle-scarred bull elephant-seals
shaped and sized much like your little finger
would let themselves be cradled in the gentle
soothing arms of tall elegiac sea-horses who'd
perambulate across the rippling wet sand
in gingham and Flemish lace, conversing
about the real world of wakefulness where
families war and nations hate in the evolving
ebb and flow of developing consciousness;
and the time-transcending generations of gender
across species and life-form would be patterned
to include awareness of our identity as a choice
not an imposition; and the unbearable extent
of grief and loss would be understood to mean
that loving and knowing another completely
enables death to become an intense golden
encircling of self; the androgynous starfish
could then warm up enough to allow itself a sex;
after that the tide could turn and tip the ocean in
again over everything, washing all of it away

Mnemonic

Although its surely true that really you
are flapping around fearfully like the wings
of a broken bird at the moment,

it is nevertheless sometimes worth
staying still, and pretending all is well
– preening, puffing up, acting smug

and self-effacing at one and the same time,
determined to face all your inevitabilities
despite not knowing what they really are.

It enables them to take colour, and shape
into perfectly formed little eggs for you
to nest your life around

if you don't toss them over and out; your
warmth will then find them hatching soft
and downy or scaled and hard, but new

and longing to be loved unconditionally
in the warm wet nourishment of being,
named for what and who they are by you.

And don't worry if you don't know what
makes a serpent different from a sparrow –
after all, fangs can sing and beaks can bite;

and anyway even when they actually can't
all you have to do is let yourself learn
to love what you have no control over.

Not just because it helps to shape you,
but also because everything is here for you
to help give shape to too. But if I sound

over-confident, please ignore my clumsy
unsubtle proselytising. I know, I do know
there's nothing more stupid than certainty.

zcary

The howling grunting mewling moon
Curls up in my heart like a lap cat napping
Pretending to sleep as it bleeds white
Shite blood all over my anguish;
Till I fly, cackling like a witch,
Over all the angry bubblings troubling
My tenderness. Then wealing gashes
Take shape perfectly to fit
My mother's soft suck-kissing lips.
Each one sliced precisely down
To the tendons in my alabaster wrists,
Branding my flesh all over as hers.
Even as she washes it with her tears.
Her smiles which were as perfect
As her Rimmel-red finger nails,
As genuine as powdered infant-formula,
And as regular as my three-hourly feeds,
Were made of drug treatment for abuse.
But our sweet consolation was
(is and always shall be) that she needed me.
Her traced scratch became my gaped slash –
My stifled screech the music in her soul.
Happily, ever after she had hurt me
She would soothe me in her camisole
And I would pretend to sleep.
Now, although livid blood is seeping
Through and staining my calico
And I am never able to cry anymore,
Nevertheless, I know who I am alright:
I used to see my reflection in the moon
Which was my mirror, you see, till I
Broke it. (I dropped it and it shattered –
Silly me!) So if I sometimes have to swallow
The shards, so what? I have taken her
To heart. That's all. And I just can't stomach
All that lunatic babbling all the time.
Otherwise I'm completely fine, thank you.
Really!!! So is mum. We both are.

Waterfall

emotion swirling in eddies of longing
batter and bruise us both as if we were
not rocks and as if we felt everything
which spills over and passes through

us; my need for you has emptied my
stomach all over the parquet floor
and when you shout at me your
words merge with my tinnitus

and I would want to run away
if my legs wouldn't shake like this
all the time; it feels like feeling
will break me up and wash me away

so that I am diluted biochemically
into homeopathic elements and slipped
into your cordial for you to sip
at your leisure if only you

were not becoming hole-riddled too;
look at us, we are hardly recognisable
and neither of us knows who we
are anymore but still we go on,

even as we are disintegrated
and swept downstream by all
the reasons and blame we cannot
own, still we go on churning

out the same old redundant shapes
and patterns; we will become
ghosts, bantams perpetually shrieking
at the lux aeterna for not shining

here, as if what has happened was
nothing to do with us, as if we could
not help it, as if we had no choice,
as if emotions erode who we are

like water channelling out its
own route to wherever it wants to go
without a care in the world
for anything or anyone else.

sad not depressed.

letting the rain beat your words into my head
and finally hearing them though it's too late now
and you are long gone; letting it wash down my
my forehead and face and the back of my neck
as if you were still touching me with both hands
and I was able to let you without resentment or
fear; letting memories of your caring for me have
a life I never could allow them when they were
happening; letting my regret and remorse about
that grip me epileptically in a vice around my
temples; letting myself collapse crying to the
cold wet depths that I miss you more than I care
about my life anymore; letting that overwhelm
and drown me; letting the water into my lungs
even as I fight instinctively to stop it; letting
ultimate things put me into pale perspective so
who I am doesn't matter anymore; letting my tiny
sense of self loose in time; letting myself survey
and learn from what I did and what I could do if
I lived longer; letting what you said funnel me
spiralling into a little death which can unfasten and
detach me from all of it so that I simply merge with
your words; letting language itself find what it
means to be a person even as I come into not being
one anymore; letting discourse just be between
people, ordinary and everyday, but simultaneously
and secretly another universe rippling and shaping
itself into existence; just letting go of everything
except connectedness with that, and with you,
and with what you said which was you loved me.

opal

As relentless as time, coldest, darkest winter winds hit
The water horizontally, whiting it; and I was tossed
Flotsam being smashed into insignificance by rolling
Waves of angry isolation. Lost on the rocks where all
Angles are hard, oppositional and acute; it was the noise
Which was intolerable, not the pain, as I crashed again
And again, against the fact of my self cutting and scouring
All my surfaces on pointed jagged truths which were
Bloodily scraping away all the sweet conceits and great
Pretensions which till now had always been 'me'. It hurt,
It hurt to be battered and broken in harsh mindless rows of
Charging, churning forward rolls, over and over, then down
Into seething undertows sucking me back out again. I bit
Off my lip but did not cry out as my raw salted flesh and
Broken bones were grated and ground down. I gurgled.
I choked. The end closed in. And then I think I drowned.

Which was okay because I found myself lying on soft
Sand, beached and steaming quietly beneath the warm
Sun of an uncannily calm, late summer day. The gently
Lapping sea was the colour of mist, but clearer than a bell
A new born baby walked across it towards me, delighted
To see me as if I was hers and we belonged to one another.
Caught in her light I sat up smiling, forgetting all that had
Gone before. Far too young to be walking yet the baby danced
Knowingly across the water and threw herself into my arms.
Instinctively I embraced her, cradling her tininess tenderly,
Even looking around for something to wrap her in. I was
Just entranced as she looked me straight in the eyes, taking
Me for granted and knowing me at one and the same time.
Then I looked up. I saw that the sky had become golden and
Somehow we had switched – she was holding me, murmuring
Everything was alright. I felt so safe I suckled. Then I slept.

Bananas split

She draws herself out from inside,
Riling him with the shape of her feelings,
Flooding him with them till he fears he will drown.

He just wants her to leave him.
To go. It is as if she was all around
Him and inside him, taking him over as if she were a man.

He tries to withdraw into himself, to
Learn to swim within; either that or to construct
A fabulous palace of thoughts to tower over her emotion.

She is certain that they know of
No alternative to their inter-dependence –
The trouble is he always denies that. Like she wasn't there.

And of course in principle it is just
Possible that their mutual need for each other
Is a fantasy, that he's right, she actually does need to go

To test it out. But his refusal to let her
Have anything other than a masturbatory existence
Fills her with foreboding. It feels so difficult to disappear

From her own life just because he can
Not bear having her around anymore. It hurts
To be given only two choices: either to be kept inside

The whole time, his secret prisoner,
Or to be banished altogether, when she knows
That means they'll both die. It makes no sense to do away

With herself for him, when it means
That he will die too. She screams out loud:
'How stupid this is. Why can't you just live with me, let me

Be?' But he berates her back coldly
Stating that she has never been able to share
Him without arbitrarily trying to wash him in emotions

And behaviours which she knows
Will drown him. Exasperated, she yells either
Way then, if she stays or if she goes she will kill him –

'Isn't that what you're saying? Well
I may as well stay… I love you anyway and
I would rather be with you when you die then far away.

The fit between us is dangerous.
Sanctimony and slick solutions may cover
That up, but beneath the sheets our differences connect us

Let's just stay close together. Please. If my
Feelings should flood you, you can build a tower of
Ideas for us to climb up, with a room where we can sleep'.

Gynandric 1.

the enrolment is formalised,
brutal in its tender attention to the
atrophy of feeling, and

you can understand why crocodiles
cry when their nature compels them
to devour what they have loved.

the enrolment is a terrible tearing
of the centre of who we are into
separate differentiated halves, and

you can understand why worms turn
in writhing despair to abjectly suck
the sweetness bleeding from their tails.

the enrolment confers social duties,
the dereliction of which leads to exile
from convention to derision, and

you can understand why clowns
have to paint the tears on their cheeks
before the crowd can laugh at them.

the enrolment requires a dress code of
mouth and trousers, or lipstick and prattle
to squat in for the length of a life, and

you can understand the schizophrenic
need to split off from that in the vain
hope of finding peace in confusion.

but the enrolment is compulsory and
dictates everything, from how long
you are suckled as a tiny baby

at your mothers breast through to
the way you are finally laid out
in your fabulous funeral dress.

gynandric (II).

slick
as a salamander,
and curved like the throat
of a blind woman with her head
tilted up and staring like a statue at the sun,
the dream shimmers inviolate in the day's naked light;

tantalising
the edges of your
perception with dark night time
hues, coyly trying to tell you not to look,
as rational explanations are slipped hurriedly on
like clothes when the postman is knocking at the door;

but even so
you try to grasp
what you have seen, as
if it were not a wraith, and as if
you could hold it in your hands like the stone
waist of a woman or a man with neither arms nor legs;

although actually
it has both, and is alive and
struggles and kicks and wants to
bite you till you bleed. Only then will it
take you into its arms and gently soothe your
troubled brow until you no longer know what is real.

Don't ever forget
that most dreams are
gone before you can see them,
and they will hurt you or even kill you
if you fail to remember for a moment that you
are inside them far more than they are ever inside you.

Still as stone,
the salamandered
woman's breath is warm,
her breasts the golden eyes of all
your storms, and as you climb into her arms
you find it is your very self you're blindly trying to hold.

gynandric (III)

Gendered enrolment
Is brutal in the attention
It tenders to the atrophy
Of full feeling. It is
Compulsory and it
Dictates everything
From how you were
Suckled as a baby
At your mother's breast
Through to how you are
Finally plugged
And laid to rest
In delicate tulle
And matching mules
Or a sombre suit
And lace-up shoes.

And afterwards
In your grave
The worms turn
For a little while
Between your toes,
Waiting for your ghost
To close the circle
By finding your soul.
Then they can feast
Because now
You are whole.
This is why
I often cry:
Because completeness
In this world
Can only be realised
In dreams.

Infant Song
1.

Wet-borne from the warm enclosed night
And bursting forth in blood into the light
I could only cry, trapped in the freedom
Of breathing and sucking without words,
And without knowledge of how you would
Or would not take to me. After weeks of
Breaking your back and bolstering your
Hugged holster belly with my burgeoning,
I didn't know I broke your waters or that
The midwife telling you to breathe properly
And refrain from bearing down till she told
You to, would have you heaving with a
Deeply felt resentment for the whole human
Condition, and for me in particular; as the
Concentration on trying to produce me properly
Became the single biggest thing you had ever
Known. Thus it never was a penis, it was always
This, this all-powerful, all-pain, all-consuming
Process of childbirth which really put an end to
Your virginity. I was to blame, though I didn't
Know it, because I only knew that you were my
Everything. I did not know if you would find it
In you to love me after the overwhelmingness of
My expulsion from your belly ripped and tore
Your vagina into henceforth always feeling
Never the same again. I did not know I did not
Know. I did not know anything. All I knew was
That I needed you and I did not mean my need
To seem as if you could have been anyone to me.
I meant just to be, nothing more. But even that
Didn't really seem to be a choice as I flailed
Helplessly, and began to make the tiny choked
Mewls of the newborn discovering that mouth
Means sound. Their piping wiped my uterine
Memories white-clean away, making me forget
Your soft echo-chamber womb and how very
Small, closed and enclosed it had become before
Without knowing what we did, we somehow agreed
It was finally time for me to leave. Your waves
As you ocean-poured me out from within were
So powerful that by the end both of us must have
Felt that we were dying: you were being split almost
Asunder; and when the cord slipped round my neck
I saw my whole life pass before me – stillborn.
But though my skin went blue, friendly fingers
Eased the pressure and the midwife's soothing tones
Made me want to cry. And when I was out I did. Then
I heard you sob, gasping out between your breaths
If I was alright. And when told I was, you asked what
I was. And when you were told that, you let out one
Little laugh – partly for the joy of it, and partly for
Regret. As the cord was clamped and cleanly cut, I
Was bleating. Smiling, you reached for me, crying too.

Infant Song
2.

You took me in your arms, put me to your breast,
As if that was where I had always rightfully
Really belonged; and I screwed up my sightless
Eyes, and puckered my lips as if I had always and
Only just sucked or slept. But we could not yet
Connect and you stroked my squashed head joking
That I looked alright all things considered. I didn't
Know who you were as you spoke and I looked at
You just once, a stolen glance taken in advance of
All the looks that would pass between us in future.
But you caught it and you cooed at me as if I was
Yours forever more. I shied and looked away, then
Back again unsure, unknowing, booted out forever
From your belly and just for a moment, feeling it.
I blinked, eyes rolled, rolling on the sensation of just
Lying there in your arms, separate, still, held. But it
Was all too soon to recognise and I did not know,
As I looked away and back again that you were my
Everything. I did not know anything. I did not know
Your nipple put to my gums and lips till you were
Told to place it right in and then I bit instinctively,
Tasted the essence of what was other yet fine, mother
But mine, and the whole golden world was coming
Into my mouth. And I wanted to turn my taste for it
Into words as honeyed as yours were now. So I burped
Out the last of drops from our amniotic sea mingling
With your waters of immunity now minutely clear and
Shining, heralding the imminent flow of your milk.
And I babbled a bit, roundly imagining what I saw
Before me now as your nipple dripped and met my
Dribble running in a small slow stream down the
Side of my neck making us both feel soft, sweet and
Wet. And then I was your breast and you were inside
And all around me again. Only the different light and
The sounds made me feel that there might be another
World outside and all around you. Which I could not
Comprehend; I nuzzled your breast, my eyes closed.
There was nothing beyond. Not yet. Just you for me
And me yours, alone. The stars shone in my belly
And you were the mother of the one whole universe.
I dreamed then that comfort and love conquered all
Fear and anxiety, that they simply did not exist; that
There was nothing between the stars which was not
Ours – our softness, our skin, our warmth, our holding
In of all that was perfect in mutually containing love.
The awful memory of push and pain was really now
Forgotten by both of us because both of us were one
Again. You ignored and I was ignorant of the men
And midwives still bustling about, cleaning up their
Instruments and putting them away, relaxed now
Because we were born, then moving to the woman in
The room next door who started before you but now
Urgently needed an epidural to help her stop screaming.

Engenderings

Infant Song
3.

Your sleeping was fitful, mine was as deep and as
Empty as my memory of all that had gone before.
You were kept awake by my tiny fluid-flecked
Snores and looked at my dependent otherness – how
Could I have been a part of you and yet now apart
From you keeping you awake with the regularity
Of my breathing as if air was also a mother to me?
For a moment you were jealous and your breasts
Felt heavy with the need to feed me. You shifted
Your still painful bottom on the bloodied sheets,
Trying and not trying to disturb me too. I gave an
Involuntary shudder and whimpered as a nurse
Came up smiling and asking you if we both were
Alright, bent to plump your pillow suggesting you
Knead your nipple and place it in my mouth, as you
Bent forward achingly to let her. You could tell
That though she'd said it a thousand times before
To new-born mothers, she had never had to do it
Herself or she'd know it was almost impossible
To do anything right now. And then somehow I
Was latched on, sucking your very self from
Inside you with a power and energy belying my
Hours-old existence. You swallowed your brief
Alarm and allowed yourself a smile looking down
At the magnitude of my tiny need for you. I bit you
And you yelped, pulling yourself away. I cried.
You half-cried too, apologising and telling me off
In one and the same gasp. This was getting serious,
Perhaps we two were not one after all. I cried some
More. I did not know. I did not know what was
Going on, why suddenly you were you, and you were
Doing this to me. And I wasn't a part of you after all.
I cried inconsolably. I did not know what I had done
And I did not know what was happening. All I knew
Was what I felt, and it felt unbearable. Your breast
Was in my face, squashing me, wetting me, drowning
Me. I tried to turn away but you reached round up
From under, gently pushing my head round to face
You. Jerking away and screaming now in reaction, all
I knew, and all I was, and all you were, was terrifying
And terrible. And parts of me I did not know I had –
Vocal chords, tongue, arms, legs, tummy and bum
All terrified me too with their chor-accompaniment
To my terror which was as real as your confusion.
You gathered yourself and attended to what you had
Done by trying to soothe me, rocking me in your arms
And telling me it was alright but I could not hear you;
I was shaking between screams and whooping for that
Air that had been a mother to me forgotten moments
Ago. I could sense your disturbance as you tried to lie
Me back into quiescence. I shuddered for a moment
And was still, and you sighed with relief. You slipped
Your nipple back into my mouth before again, and I
Didn't know why, I sucked, then swallowed, then slept.

Cairns Clery

Infant Song
4.

I could sense your milk within me, warm, wet and
Nourishing and moving me like I was empty inside;
As if all I was, was the sensory all-enveloping tubular
Enclosure of what I was not, which was the movement
Of what you were giving me, passing through me. I
Kept on sucking though, wanting to feel you inside
As I felt you outside and all around me. I felt as if
It was me having you in reverse; as if, by making
A mother of you I made one of myself. It felt as if
It could have been me who had just delivered you.
Although my head was the same size as your breast
I felt huge; and though tiny against it, my free hand
Patted and stroked your breast like it was a small
Thing which needed my love and care. I did not
Know I did not know that this was what I felt. I just
Felt it, and you knew it for me, smiling that all was
Well in the intimate privacy of our world of worlds
Once more. But then I felt a hiatus at the top of
My tummy, and it was all your fault for filling me
So full, and it felt so big and painful that I could
Only wheel my head back and wail as it grew huge
Inside me threatening to split open my chest and
Throttle my throat. You picked me up and held me
Upright against your shoulder and the burp welled
Up and out and over onto you. Then I collapsed
Against you, discovering gravity, the weakness of
The muscles in my neck, and relief as the antithesis
Of pain, all at the same time. You held my head,
Patted my back and I felt a downward movement
Coming in a rush as big as the burp had been and
Heard your laugh of recognition. I knew you knew
What was happening to me and I clung on to you –
Both the cause and solution to all my problems.
While I slept again, satisfied, safe in your arms
You looked at me with satisfaction yourself; you
Now knew that you could get the measure of me
And that though my need for you was utter, you
Didn't mind if it meant that you could meet it.
And now you thought you knew you could. You
Allowed yourself some confidence as you looked
At me. I was safe and tiny again having seemed so
Enormously demanding in my needs moments ago.
For the first time since I had arrived from within
You would take some time for yourself. You brushed
Your hair and made your way gingerly to the loo
Trying to imagine being how you were and who
Before me. You looked at your flushed yet washed
Out features in the mirror and smiled at the irrelevant
Memory of childlessness you tried to conjure up, now
You had me to measure it by. But it was just a feeling
You would never have again except perhaps through
Me. You made your way back to your bed and looked
Down at me, your newborn baby as wizened as an old
Person breathing their last. I woke and cried for you

69

Infant Song
5.

Your nipples were sore, both of them equally,
And I could sense you flinching and glaring at
Me and telling the nurse this was unbearable
And you'd decided that I'd do best on a bottle.
I sensed your brittle anger on being told you
Were wrong – didn't a mother know best? You
Kept on pulling away and I did too, and between
Us we were not even a little easy or content. So I
Did what I could which was to bite or to pull or
To cry, and if I'd known it, I would have known
I'd tasted blood, having made you so raw. But I
Didn't know anything except my trouble feeding
Or being comforted, and after a while, which was
Forever to me, we were both crying together.
You kept trying to wipe your tears from my cheeks
And I just bawled in a frenzy of being unfed and
Uncared for. I did not know you cared. Your tears
Were rain and so were mine and I was drowning.
You breasts were hard and full – it was as painful
To feed me as not to. Suddenly I fell asleep from
Exhaustion, without knowing it. And while I dreamed,
You tried to clean yourself and cream yourself ready
For the next onslaught. If I could have told you what
I dreamt you would have joined me for we were not
Troubled where I was: where sleep is peaceful and
Dreams are shining and as still as the breaks in our
Breath. But I could only rest till I woke even more
Fretful than before that I was the yoke chaining you
To a role you did not want anymore. My cries became
Feeble and you gritted your teeth and shut your eyes,
Trying one last time to feed me. For a blissful moment
It was heavenly and I forgot the pain panging
My whole belly, and your ariolae felt anaesthetised.
But then I started drowning again and I spat you out
Choking. For one mad moment you wanted to hit me.
But there was no respite for either of us. I screamed
As you sobbed and neither of us knew how it was
That just as we had both given up we were somehow
Reconnected. I was sucking contentedly and you
Were smiling through your tears and stroking me
Like I was your dear one all over again. Afterwards
As I slept, you wept and wept for both of us and
Thought of all the things I would face, years ahead,
When all this terrible intimacy would one day be
Replaced by independence and fate as we let each
Other go. You imagined me as a toddler, then a
Child, as an adolescent and beyond; separate; you
An old woman, me with children of my own. And
Even as I lay there, lighter now than when I was born,
You saw all this like it had already happened. And
Then you wanted to kill me, to crush me in your arms
With your love, protect me from all the awful things
I'd have to live through without you there to help me.
Then I softly squirmed in my sleep and you shivered.

Cairns Clery

Infant Song
6.

Sleep was sweet succour too. For both of us. We
Would return to where we came from, knowing,
And at peace, with all things. The rhythmical
Regularity of our separate breathings would
Harmonise – mine twice as fast as yours, as though
I had so much catching up to do. Your breasts
Reflected this, filling up and feeling lumpen and
Hard when I didn't wake up to feed. You felt like
Some strange six thousand year old fertility goddess,
Fetished into a purely feeding shape, while I slept
On oblivious. A nurse told you they would settle
Down, don't worry. You smiled gratefully, hating
Her. When I finally awoke I added insult to injury,
Wanting not to find you, but only to search. And I
Worked myself into another frenzy after pushing you
Away, then sucking you in after all, then immediately
Choking on your over-fullness and spitting you out
Again, seemingly bent on repeatedly getting it all
Wrong, again and again. But I now knew that I did
Not know. And I looked for you everywhere, howling
My need as your blue breasts screamed to feed me.
Right in front of my face. Then, as before, I was on
Again without either of us quite knowing how, and
Your milk streamed straight down my throat like a
Sweet, unstoppable, swollen molten river at its estuary.
And my mouth and belly were the sea. All I was was
In my lips and tongue and tum, tucked in your arms,
Snug, warm, wanting for nothing. You wondered at
How we could move from infinite heaven to eternal
Hell and back again in an instant. I simply sucked.
Sometimes I would just stop, as if wondering about
It myself, then start again with renewed vigour till
The trapped air in my tummy got too much and you
Had to put me over your shoulder again. And all the
While I started to know that I knew a little. I began
To know your different murmurings and mutterings
As you shifted to make us more comfortable, or
Bustled around me, having put me down to change
My nappy. And I could smell your scent as you bent
To attend to me. You were like music with your
Melodic repetition of everything you felt for me
Enfolding itself around our relationship and calling
Up an answering tune in me. Slowly I knew that I
Was beginning to make it out. As we lay in the dark
Still night together, you drifting in and out sleep, me
Attached to your nipple and sucking on you feverishly
Whenever you moved, it was as if I sensed now that I'd
One day lose this intimacy with you for what would be
Ever after ever after that. For now though, all I knew
Was I needed you. And as you rested your hand on my
Tiny back I could almost feel your need for me too – to
Milk you. I burped over you bringing some up. Then you
Groaned and reached for a tissue from under your pillow

Engenderings

Infant Song
7.

To wipe yourself with, while I lay happily on my back
Babbling, jerking, gesticulating importantly, like I
Was interesting, and genuinely interested in sharing
The small hours with you. You did not know whether to
Laugh or cry, exhausted in the nether of the night, as I
Lay there wide awake and alert to every nuance of your
Being; as if the wisdom of ages had opened my eyes
So that I could see everything you thought and felt.
For a moment you were almost shy as I seemed to
Stare right into you, but then you relaxed, sensing
It was a trick of the moonlight filtering onto my face.
All I could see was your boobs bobbing before me,
And I even seemed to see them when they weren't
Actually there – you came back from the loo to find me
Busily waving at them and patting them and sucking
At them in my excited imagination. You slipped back
Into bed beside me and met it with the fact a second
Before it could dawn on me that I had been sucking on
Air, and I took you in to my mouth like you had always
Been there, and I did not see your secret knowing smile.
But all the time now, not so secretly, I began to know
What to expect from you. I could tell what mood you
Were in just by looking up at you as I fed, feeling the
Emotional state you were in by the way you held me
In your arms. I could tell when you were relaxed and
Had all the time in the world to attend to me. I could
Tell when you were abstracted, tense and hurried, and
I found I could not get a proper grip on your nipple at
Such times and you would get irritated with me, trying
To attach me as if I was a button you wanted to do up.
I could tell when you were depressed, your breasts sore,
The cupboard empty, the clothes dirty, the home a mess,
And it was all my fault. You would go through all the
Motions with me, doing everything you needed to do.
But without being able to love, it was all to no avail and
I could feel myself ailing because there was no light in
Your smile. I grizzled and cried more, trying to ignore
You, to become and remain self-contained, as if our
Six week old relationship was sixteen years and I could
Fend for myself thank you very much. You noticed my
Miniscule stand-offishness and made such a fuss of
Me that I gave you my first deliberate smile. It came
Rising out of me like a burp or the sun at dawn, without
Either of us knowing it was going to, till there it was.
You laughed; your delight was palpable and I gave you
Another one. Then you picked me up and hugged me,
Dancing around the room, kissing me excitedly and
Exclaiming on what I'd done till I brought my milk back
Up over your freshly laundered dress. Then you put me
Back down with what was almost a bump and started to
Cry. Soon we were both howling in that way we would
Get to know so well as the months went by. Eventually
Your face hardened and you decided to leave me to it.

Cairns Clery

Infant Song
8.

I knew how to cry. I thought I knew too that you
Would come to me when I called, because you always
Had before. When I forgot what I knew because
All I was, was the tightness in my chest and the hole
In the heart of my head where you had always been
Before and from where all of me was now feeling
Shattered, I could not bear it. My cries turned to
Glass, fractured, clear and sharp. I felt broken, cut
Transparently into shards by your awful absence.
I did not know you felt it was best to leave me to cry
Now, so that I would learn that I did not just 'have
You on tap', that that was what your mother had
Said to you would be 'best for both of you, dear, in
The long run'. I did not know you were just outside
My door biting your lip and trying to force yourself
To hear me and not respond, feeling my every tear
As if it was your own. When my cries became weak,
Breathless whimpers you could take no more and
Came running back to me, pouring out your sorrow
For what you had done, unhooking your bra and picking
Me up all in one movement and crushing me against
Your flesh like you would never let go of me again.
I didn't know what or who either of us was. I wasn't
Frantic or rejecting. I wasn't anything. I didn't feel.
It was as if I had just been born again or had just died.
Your cuddling of me was meaningless as my breast
Heaved and spasmed. I sighed and fell asleep without
Feeding, for the first time. You wouldn't put me down,
Continued holding me against you, resting your arm
Against the side of the chair not daring to disturb me.
You wondered how your mother could ever have done
Such a thing to you, stroking the side of my face.
A film of dribble and sweat separated us. Carefully
You shifted position to be ready to put your nipple to
My mouth when I awoke. But I didn't. I seemed to
Be sleeping forever, tiny beads of sweat peppering my
Forehead and cheekbones. For a moment, as you looked
Down at me you could see the trappings of babyhood –
Pudgy cheeks, button nose – fall away and I looked just
Like you. People had already remarked as such, as
People do, but now you saw it for yourself and you
Vowed to yourself, as people do, that you would never
Do that again, that leaving a baby to cry is cruel. You
Felt that you would never have done it if I had still been
Newborn, but to have repaid my first smile with an
Angry absence just because I'd messed your dress was
Unbelievably petty and selfish. Remorse felt, well, it
Felt appropriate. You were not going to treat me like
You were treated yourself. That was the last thing you
Would want to do. When I did finally stir it was as if
The whole incident had never happened. I had plainly
Only remembered your givingness because I immediately
Latched onto you again, glugging milk down contentedly.

Infant Song
9.

Your relief was tinged with depression because you
Knew the road to hell is paved with good intentions,
And all these baby-focussed days and nights were
Beginning to be wearisome. I stopped suckling and
Opened my eyes, sensing your uncertainty again, and
Feeling that you both loved me and hated me. To
Look at you was suddenly to see myself, and I blinked
At the beauty of our reflection as I poohed noisily.
We smiled simultaneously, which made us both smile
Some more. For a while we were completely at one
With one another, and I loved your loving me totally
And unconditionally. There was no before or after.
There was only now. I touched your mouth and you
Sucked on all four of my fingers. When you moved
To stop I kept my hand up wanting more. But you
Put me down and I could hear you talking differently.
I didn't know you were on the phone but I knew you
Were still about and I lay still looking and listening.
I could tell you were not happy by the tone of your
Voice which made me unhappy too. Then I wanted
You back and called for you, but you did not come.
You started speaking defensively as if being attacked,
And it felt like it was me who had upset you. I began
To cry and I heard you say 'it's not *the* fucking baby –
It's our fucking baby' and put the phone down sadly.
You picked me up trying to console me but now I had
Worked myself up into a state of agitation which you
Instinctively recoiled from, going off to fetch another
Nappy, not meaning to leave me to cry. But the phone
Rang again – I recognised the sound – and you must have
Answered it elsewhere because you didn't come back,
And I could not hear your voice this time. All I could
Hear were my own fearful cries which consumed me
With their noise and power, so that once again there
Was nothing else beyond what I felt. And my feelings
Were what I was and what I was, was upset and bereft.
I choked on my own screaming and sicked up all of
What you had given me. Lying in my vomit crying, I
Wanted to stop, and started banging my head on the
Side of my cot as if it would hurt me not to. I was a
Drum beating out the time of my distress to the rhythm
Of my cries. When you did eventually return I had no
Knowledge of what was happening or who you were.
I did not notice you were crying too. I did not see that
In your unhappiness you could not cope with mine.
You tried to shush me but I was utterly inconsolable
And you were too. This time you did not leave me to
Cry, you just cried too, till we were both so exhausted
That it just petered out into an apathy which we would
Both be wont to share more and more of as time went
By. You couldn't be bothered to change my nappy now.
We both went to sleep side by side, feeling hopeless and
Alone, and like we didn't know that the other was there.

Infant Song
10.

Lying in shit leaves you feeling sore. The cheeks
Of my bum felt raw, and when you tiredly turned
To tend to them your exclamation at their redness
Would have been ashamed had your feelings not
Been dulled by the combination of seeing to me
Whilst being vilified and abused yourself. The purple
Bruises on your arms and abdomen were nothing to
To do with my being born some three months before.
You washed me and slapped some cream on, ignoring
My pitiful pained cries. You told me disconsolately
It was best to let you get on with it and I'd be glad of
It later. I would have been angry at your unfeeling
Attitude if I had been more robust, and if I had been
Older I might have understood the mirrored brutal
Insensitivity you were reflecting on me, but all I knew
Was what you were doing to me and how you were
Doing it. I hated how I hurt and how you didn't seem
To care but I couldn't look at you reproachfully because
I knew that without you I was nothing. After you were
Done and I was all clean and changed, I didn't want
To look at you and now I could use my neck muscles
I could turn away. So I did, but also because you were
Crying again. For a moment I wanted to comfort you,
Be mother, tell you everything was going to be alright,
But I was too little to know anything beyond this was
What I felt. I couldn't even say 'mama' yet, although
On good days you had recently begun to get me to try,
Mimicking my noises and developing them to sound like
Yours. So I just closed down, autistically ignoring you,
Ignoring my feelings and concentrating instead on the
Sensations in my body. I poohed again. You heard me
And smelled me and having just finished seeing to me
The prospect of starting all over again was too much.
You yelled angrily, sweeping out of the room. When
You came back I had fallen on the floor, grown ten feet
Tall and taken a shape with which to devour you. My
Left shoulder was on fire and while it burned me up
I screeched and clawed at you. You winced warily trying
To stay out of my reach. I had no legs just yet and big
As I was I could not really move, but my maw was wide
Enough to swallow both of us whole, and I could tell
By the frightened look in your eyes that I would. I was
Kali'd, an angry wounded destroyer of worlds, and having
Done that to yours it felt the only kind thing would be
To eat you too. And if I added your skull to my necklace
It would be the centrepiece. And I would always be you
Really, loving and hating me and holding you to my
Tender bosom like I was a precious jewel. Transfixed
By shock you just stopped and watched me for a moment
Screaming on the floor, then rushed to pick me up, and
Then I became tiny again in your arms, desperate for your
Love.You checked me over and decided I was alright, had
Not broken anything. Our mutual embrace was absolute.

ALEXITHYMIC

Spanning a metre or more
my moth mother looms huge,
black and epileptic blue,
across the self-slung glutinous
mud of my cysting volcano.

Indifferent to me she is
fanning my fury back into life
by whirring her gleaming
petal flesh wings powder dry.
Then I see her rising anciently

up into my sight to disturb
my eyes with her absolute
otherness. And as they blink
I am muttering in disbelief
at her suddenly sinking again,

soundless and batfish-quick
into their pupil'd enquiry;
lodging with barely a flutter
deep down behind my brain
as quiet and dark as night,

and henceforth visible only
in dreams. So I send for sleep
and aeons pass geologically
slow yet darting needle fast,
identical with instants.

Silent orgiastic shudders
occasionally spray pupae into
my cerebellum, but there is no
other sign of her existence
nor of her neonates' secret

development munching
my hippocampus like lettuce
and patterning it with future
contradictions – still-births,
the wisdom of madness,

machine-tooled feelings, that
kind of thing. Now I might be
silly or simply confused but
I would just love to take a
a shining hammer and a long

sharp nail and impale the moth
still flapping, to my temple,
a floppy reminder that I too
can and do spring surprises.
But actually, I think, I won't.

Bleat the Retreat

Sticking rigidly
to redundant patterns,
the shape-maker's imagination
is circumscribed
by dimensionality,
colour and form.
Structurally,
all the worlds
are held together
by this vision of matter
which takes no cognizance
of insubstantial things
like feelings.

What can not
be sensed
cannot exist,
is the gist –
without an evidence base
there is no proof
of anything.
That this itself
is merely a belief
isn't recognised
because beliefs
are as insubstantial
as smoke.
And I Am Burning.

Despair prayer

Where

It's not

Cliffed,

Vertical,

Holdless

And in my face,

My consciousness

Is chasmed

Devoid

Of foreseen

Bottomless

Black holes.

It's a trap

With a cheese.

I'm a mouse.

Kill me please.

I promise

I'll not mix

My metaphors

Again.

Ever.

Summer isle

The cairn I built
On Taeg na bhair
Bit the wind
And shaped it into
Shimmying invisibly
In different directions
As it made its
Point. Neither
Sheep nor rabbits
Pastured there
But if they had
They would have felt
How the wind
Screamed to be still
And chased them
hurrying off down
To somewhere
More sheltered.
They would have
Known that
The beautiful forlorn
Mountains and sea
Around them
Were there for them
To find the safety
Of solitude upon,
And then they'd
Have scurried
Down the peaty paths
Again to mingle
Once more
With their loved ones
And friends,
Not speaking
Of what they had seen
And felt.
Just letting it be,
Munching the tufted
Grass with teeth
Made for tearing
And forgetting about it
Till the next time
They happened
To wander that way.

Aortal optic

the eyes in my heart
are beyond me,
they are and are not mine,
but it really does not matter
because really
really I'm really fine

the eyes in my heart
are all-seeing
which soothes
the wounds
in my soul.
my sliced up thoughts
and feelings,
are gently bathed
by their gaze

so when little things
mean far too much,
or massive things
nothing at all,
what it does discreetly
is put them
back in place

the eyes in my heart
could see me
before I ever was born,
and now they see me
struggling still, trying
not to be torn

by how painful
life can feel,
trying just to look
and trying just to see.

hypnogogic

As soon as I started to sleep
the walls of my room fell away
merging with warm blue skies
and as yet uncut childhood meadows
gently humming
in early summer sunshine.

I was skirting my secret
sadness in a floral fuck
over the exposed
surfaces of my skin.

First I butter-cupped
the wounds I'd made earlier
on my arms
in bright yellow and green
sleeves of stems
and petals and leaves.

Then I knelt my grubby
and purposeful little knees
on purple thistles
which peppered them
all over with tiny red pricks.

Finally I washed my face
with nettles, pretending
they were soap, till it shone
full of whorls and weals
pink, white, and neat as pins.

Then I found I was putting on
a pastoral for you, mother,
making up
a dance to divert you
from the humourless farce
you were in;

and for you father
so that you might just once
see something other
than the roundness of her arse.

But I failed to get your notice
so I gave you mine;
and the fallow fields of my dream
stood up again
and I found myself back, staring
at the cold walls of adult insomnia.

82

exclusive chain

when you can only feel
you cannot
think;
when you can only think
you cannot
imagine;
when you can only imagine
you cannot
speak;
when you cannot speak
no one can understand;
when no one understands
you are all alone,
with only your feelings
for company
and you cannot think.

baked

When things are good I take off.
It's a recurring dream – walking
just above the ground, unweighted,
finding I go wherever I am wanted
with no friction.

A different dream is calling me now,
one in which I am
destinationed and driving
down a sandy-banked country road
which narrows

into a single track.
I should be frantic. I have lost
my husband, and a man
with eyes like arseholes encrusted
with dirt is blocking my way,

sitting on his truck waiting
for me to reverse, get out of his way,
so that he can drive past
with a leering knowing stare
to dump his load of hard core.

But he is the one who gives way
without even giving me a glance;
he backs down the way he came
pulling into the side
and allowing me to pass by.

As I raise my hand to thank him
I see that his shit-covered eyes
are turned inwards
wrapt around the deep dark mystery
of what it means to be,

oblivious of me and all my conceits.
Then carless, I lose my sense of
who I am looking for, or why, or
where I am, or anything, and I feel
the loss physically all over my body.

So I try to touch myself to make sure
I am still there, and find I am the air
holding up my husband as he flies
in his dreams just above the ground.
But I can take him wherever I want!

bauble

fed up fighting the soft illusory sheen
of necklaced feelings encircling my life
since I sat in my mother's lap, I yearn

for the reality of relationship to suddenly
loosen it like a string of pearls clattering
across the floor of dreams around me;

and I wish I did not care to be found
head down with my bottom in the air
looking for every last bead in the dark

nooks and secret crannies surrounding
me below; I wish I did not hope and pray
for help and the hand of human kindness

to guide and caress me into changing
from a small frightened hider and seeker
into an altogether finer thing – a finder

and keeper of emotions and relatedness.
I would stroke each pearl I picked up and
gently breathe warmth and recognition

back into it before rethreading it on my
string, a simple thing uncultured and freed
from all my neurotic translucent finishes –

perfectly round, perfectly formed, perfect,
as smooth and sweet as a baby babbling with
milky contentment in her havening cradle.

Beholden

The bearer of the egg
was fathered by all three
of the wise monkeys,
but was always in absolute
opposition to them.

Resisting her mummification
felt awkward and elongating
as she danced and twisted,
still elegant as a dream,
with a fertile gaping hole
between her temporal lobes.

Despite her disabilities
she could still hear my bland
securely rational refusal
to have anything to do with
the impossible task
of trying to understand.

She could see my frightened
yet complacent attachment
to the safe, sexy satisfactions
to be had from ignoring
the secret call from within.

So throwing up her hands
and twirling away
almost contemptuously
she made to leave, saying
"without your conflicts
you aren't yourself.
It's as simple as that."

Hurry!

Don't delay, don't waste a minute!
Time will hold you till yours has come
whether you wait or whether you run,
You ignore this warning at your peril.
Don't let death-fear cause you to dawdle,
or wallow in anxious self-importance
like me. Dying is a living thing touching
us all. It's in life that choices like chisels
change and shape the face of creation,
and make it eternal. When you dare take
them. So make what you will of what you
can, and what you can of what you will.
Never mind ignominy or failures, they
will provide the backdrop for what works.
Only be wary of what will wound the ones
you love – when you cannot care for them
then your connection with what matters is
blown and you are chaff in the wind of easy
options. All the world is otherwise yours.

Twelve Days in Winter

1.

(on the first day of Christmas my true love sent to me a partridge in a pear tree)

When you spoke to me
I could feel the roots
Of the pear tree
Spreading beneath us,
Reaching to feed from
Our bodies and minds

Like we were already
Dead and under the earth.
As we huddled beneath
Its leafless canopy
You told me what I already
Knew, and yet I heard it

For the very first time.
I cried as you took me
Into your arms, knowing
It could be you being held
By me. And your free hand
Gently massaged

My temple. I looked up
At the branches above
Bracing and shaping themselves
Into the unknown, searching
The lowering sky for the
Light of the long absent sun.

We were shivering then,
And shaking, when the tree
Burst into flames
Seeking to set fire
To the dark angry clouds
Rolling in from the waste.

Entranced, I reached out
For the beautiful flightless
Bird that had alighted
Beside us. With golden eyes
And honey-coloured feathers,
It spread each of its wings,

Gathering us to its breast
As if we were chicks,
And folded them around us.
Then it didn't matter anymore
That we would all be meat
For God's gaping maw.

2.
(on the second day of Christmas my true love sent to me two turtle doves)

Two turtle doves
Sat pretty,
Perched on the tip
Of the tree top
Swaying
In the wind

Borne
In time
With no memory
Of before
Or knowledge
Of after;

Asked only
To intuit
That this attested
To the truth
That the infinite
Contained them.

It was evident
That they were
Entirely easy
With everything
The tempest
Would toss at them

Even the truth
That the tenderest
Moments
Are too few
And the most terrible
Too many.

In the now
They knew
That there is
And can be
No more
Than this.

3.

(on the third day of Christmas my true love sent to me three French hens)

And there we were,
Like three French hens
Gabbling and enjoying
Ourselves hugely as if
There was no tomorrow,
Whiling ourselves away.

Me, You, and Me Too
Talking about our perceptions
And about how others see us,
Like nothing was as important.
Except that one of us
Was as cocky as a cucumber

And kept on trying
Not to be sliced by the acuity
Of the other two
As they kept on being
Right about everything.
Ducking and weaving

And always torn unnecessarily
Between fight or flight
As if their words were
Sticks and stones
Whose truth would break
The back of every bone

Stiffening my resolution.
You would touch me
Tenderly with your smiles
Trying gently to let me know
We are all from the stars
And needn't fear who we are.

But Me Too always knew
That though this was true
The loneliest lowliest part
Of darkest space where
Your shining will not be seen,
Can be a place of detachment

And despair. And no amount
Of pretending otherwise
Can change that. Turning to me
You said you'd always understood this
And I must therefore do whatever
I needed to get reconnected.

We all felt better again after that,
And re-grouping, continued to chat
About our experience and feelings
Knowing that each of us
Had given something of ourselves
To the other. And lost it too.

4.

(on the fourth day of Christmas my true love sent to me four collie birds)

Four collie birds
mean nothing to me.
I think of dreams
and great bearded storks
doggedly pretending
to be Father Christmas,

bringing babies
in their beaks like
handbags hanging
from their jowls.
But the babies
are miscarried,

And the storks
are transformed
into horses whose
hooves pound
apocalyptically,
beyond understanding,

their riders
impervious to the
particulars
of human feeling,
bent only on ending
it all for everyone.

And I know
not just that there is
no shame in crying,
but rather
that it would be
shameful not to.

So four collie birds
mean nothing to me –
not hopes extinguished,
nor love destroyed,
nor anything.
Absolutely nothing.

5.

(on the fifth day of Christmas my true love sent to me five gold rings)

The first golden ring was a doorbell peeling
Insistently as I leaned upon it desperate to be
Allowed in to the house of human life
So that I could experience helplessness,
Dependency, development and death,
And learn what love and feeling really are.

When the door opened I became an infant held
To my mother's breast. The second golden ring
Then formed around us, glowing, glistening,
And growing. Haloed by our own relationship,
We immersed ourselves in the closeness of care
Till we learned what love and feeling really are.

The third golden ring was saturnine, encircling
My persisting sense of self with experiences which
Had beginnings and ends and which I consumed
So voraciously I sometimes did not see it was my
Own children I was eating and that I was only
Here to learn what love and feeling really are.

The fourth gold ring was on the third finger of my
Love's left hand. I would often be blind to it as we
Boxed one another, when our gloves were off
And we didn't care what damage we did. But then
I would see it gleaming or grime-ridden and recall
I'd come to learn what love and feeling really are.

The fifth and final golden ring gathered together
All the things that had ever happened and spiralled
Them into the moment of departure with an intensity
As absolute as arrival once had had; and as I went with
Them they were changed for having been recognised as
Opportunities to learn what love and feeling really are

6.

(on the sixth day of Christmas my true love sent to me six geese a-laying)

When I was six,
six goose-mothers,
all breasts, bums, and feathers,
sat still with their eyes wide open
staring quietly inwards
at their own sensations,

which were contracting them
into laying eggs
any one of which could be golden
or broken
or perfectly ordinary just like them.
And I envied them

for their calm acceptance
of what life required them to do.
I felt like wringing their necks too
for the way the cold mattered
not a jot to them
so long as their eggs stayed warm.

Freezing, I wanted them to sit
on me till I could hatch,
to stay with me
till I could grow
and then to fly with me
through the winter's dusk

into my own maturity.
So I honked loudly
goose-stepping angrily
back home across the park
to my mother who gave me
a roasting for being back so late.

But when I'd warmed up
I built a little nest of twigs
I'd collected from the garden
and rolled a plasticine egg.
I sat on it and nothing my mum
could say would make me move.

7.
(on the seventh day of Christmas my true love sent to me seven swans a-swimming)

Their presence and pristine grandeur daunted me
as they sailed serene and indifferent across the
cold dark water, whiter than ice and absolutely
other. Now some ugly ducklings never grow up,
and in my neediness I knew this to be only too
true of me. Still, you can only really be jealous

of what you might have yourself, and so it was
ever so easy to genuinely admire them too, as they
glided away with understandably dismissive
huffs from my breadlessness. But one of them
stayed behind and I started thinking about sex and
identity. And almost instantly we swapped lives.

Seeing where my addled mind had idly wandered
the swan-person walked me back home imagining,
(not unreasonably), that desires must have wings
which could take me where and whenever I wanted,
and that 'home' must then be the perfect haven
where desires and their objects really come together.

While I, all unreason, dithered panicking, then hurried
to join up with the six other swans, paddling with a
chaotic lack of certainty or direction, uncomfortably
aware of the ticks beneath my wings. I took no time to
think. Perhaps the sweat I raised sent unwanted signals
to the others, because the largest one smacked his wings

and proceeded summarily to mount me without
a bye or a leave or any knowledge on my part
that it was about to occur till it happened. Glancing
anxiously from left to right in case anyone was
looking, I wanted to emit an undignified squawk
but before I could do so, he was off me again.

In the meantime the swan who had taken me home
looked out from my window at the grey leaden sky
and yearned awfully to return to her chill black waters.
Sitting down on my bed she sifted through my shiny
books and rummaged through my papers as if
somehow she thought she might find being human

more bearable if she did so. She had read them all
within minutes and found herself trembling with
the shock of finding that words were never wet
nor their meanings water for her to dive deep into.
She made my throat throb repeatedly with a sound
between a moan and a bark and rushed me back out

again to the riverside. When she called me to come
back across the water so that we could revert to our own
selves again, I wouldn't. I refused. I don't know why.
Now I am always extremely careful about accepting food
from strangers, always hiding behind the others, staying
well away from the banks. But the other six don't mind.

8.

(on the eighth day of Christmas my true love sent to me eight maids a-milking)

Nanny goats smell sweetly, tread carefully,
and know – just so – how to be discreet
yet demanding at one and the same time.
But the billy goat is rank, sackfuls of socks
have less odour, and only wants one thing:
more. More food, sex, attention, fights.

The great divide across the species is sexual.
He looks at them looking at him by way of
All the differences which draw them to him
And shows them his beard and his horns, yet
Again. Even though they may be bored by
Now they can't stop themselves looking

And longing for reconciliation which is more
Than a momentary fuck followed by a glad if
Brief return to desire-free normality; so that
They can get on with the business of caring for
The kids and talking about things that matter,
Like how to look after them and how to look

After themselves, without compromising either.
Across the way the billy goat quite shamelessly
Aspires to god-and-child-like powers by having
His cake and eating it too. He proudly proclaims
That even if he tried he couldn't do any different.
You've only got one life, and selfishness is vital

If you are not to end it frustrated and embittered.
But I'll do what I can to look after you all, of
Course I will, he says, sitting on his haunches
And cleaning his genitals with his tongue. Just
Then the milk maids come in and corral him in
His pen. Then they sit down beside the nannies

And rare morning sunshine comes streaming in
On them through the open doors. The expression
On their faces is kindly and purposeful, and they
All understand the task is one of nurturing and
Caring for the sake of it, irrespective of how they
Or the little ones eventually turn out. The billy

Goat grimaces, his front feet up on the fencing,
Watching closely, seeing nothing. Hearing the
Milk splashing into the buckets, and the kids
Bleating, but listening not at all. Musty thoughts
Of mountain ridges in spring remind him that if
They didn't live on a farm, his enthusiasms would

Not be bound by redundant self-interest and greed.
He would be governed by interest in the self and
And the need to forage just to live. Knowing he is
Just being used is something he is unable to accept
Without mad delusions of grandeur to sustain it.
It's a terrible sacrifice just wanting more. And more.

9.

(on the ninth day of Christmas my true love sent to me nine ladies waiting)

I'm always having to live in hope, she moaned, that he
Will change, find some ease with himself which is
Genuine, not based on instant gratification, like sex
With me. But why do you let him, another one asked,
If he cannot be the person you want now, he never will
Be. Waiting for someone else to change is futile. It's

A way of avoiding changing yourself – the only person
I'm waiting for is myself. Though sometimes I do worry
I'll never actually arrive. A third one said that she would
Always prefer to wait on another because she felt certain
That when our lives are over what will matter most was
Whether we were able to serve someone else's needs

Without thought of reward or personal gain. Isn't that
A contradiction said the fourth. It's like you are saying
That in the sight of God no reward is itself the reward.
What I am waiting for is death. I'm not being morbid
Or trying to avoid living, but in the end we are here to
Live and then to die. Which is why I think it's true what

They say about the good dying young. And before you
Ask, I will be eighty-one next birthday! The fifth said
We've got no choice anyway. We are all waiting whether
We like it or not. Yes, said the sixth, but at least we can
Divert ourselves while we do so, do something else to
While away the time. The seventh said anyway she liked

Waiting, it gave her time to think about her feelings and
What it all means, but the eighth disagreed saying you
Can do that without feeling you have to hang around
Through the length of your life like a wallflower. Finally,
The ninth bemoaned the lack of public toilet facilities and
Said she'd wet herself if this queue didn't start moving.

10.
(on the tenth day of Christmas my true love sent to me ten lords a-leaping)

I leafed through the lives of my lords
looking for the one which best had been me.
But they were all of a muchness
and I couldn't decide.
I'd done dangerman, strangerman, sickman
and sadman, feyman, fuckman, funnyman

and dustman. Imam and dimman.
And in their time they had all been decorated
for services rendered, above and beyond
the call of duty to the eternal state
of my uncertainty,
lauded

for their individual efforts
despite their lack of depth.
But they never learned to leap
from role-play to real play
so that the sharp edge of authenticity
was an awkward question mark

always hanging over them
like a guillotine.
Sod the lot of them, I thought,
I'll execute them all.
They all jumped up at that,
the very model of trembling alarm.

So I was prevailed upon to spare
just one. OK, I said, but you will have to
choose who that one should be.
And, mind, no drawing of lots!
They wailed and railed at that
but to their credit, refused so to choose.

I therefore amalgamated them,
squeezed them all together like putty
into one. But sadly, this one,
though heavier, was ungainly,
and even worse at leaping
into the unknown than the rest had been.

As a result
I never go out now,
which may be a bit of a shame,
but on the other hand, I suppose, I am
able, in all my empty chambers, to proclaim
that I am genuine.

11.

(on the eleventh day of Christmas my true love sent to me eleven pipers piping)

Back on the hill the burning pear tree began
To collapse into the dark smouldering night.
The icy east wind blew broken embers
Angrily across the ruins of my life in an acrid
Still glowing trail of love burnt out,
Relationship ashed, all hope smoked.

And as the wind blew it whistled like pipers
At the gates of hell queuing to send the
Woebegone down with a tune akin to the squealing
Of brakes and tyres on asphalt when a child
Is killed. Nothing could stop that wind save
Another one, but no other wind would come.

Not there where I could not even pray. Not
There where I wandered around madly as if
I could not believe what was happening,
Imagining that I was still beneath the partridge's
Wing, safe with you and with the transcendent
Power of love to triumphantly overcome

All eventualities. So I followed the windblown
Ember trail because I had no choice, accompanied
Only by the piping cacophony, but pretending
There were eleven pipers with me and I wasn't alone,
Commenting to them on how the other trees were all
Burning now, coming out in sympathy and solidarity,

Further lighting my way down into the cold dark
End of everything I'd known myself to be.
The blow which then struck me was absolute.
It was as if I didn't even feel it though I knew
That I was that child now and this was my father's car
Killing it. The detachment I then felt as I flew

From my madness was as soothing as a mother. I felt
Her take me into her arms and whisper words of love
To me, her breath holding me up in air no longer
Frozen, and gently blowing me far away from here
Into that place where understanding holds and heals
You and helps you become who you really are.

12.
(on the twelfth day of Christmas my true love sent to me twelve drummers drumming)

The hill was golden in the clear blue day
as the long-legged majorettes came dancing
down the road hurling their hoops high
in to the sky making loops around the sun.
With perfect teeth and even more perfect hair,
their delight in what they did was unconfined.

The crisp clarity of a beautiful winter's morning
contained no sign of last night's infernos, not
even a cinder; except in the expression on the
faces of the drummers who followed, grimly
rolling their sticks with a purpose and control
which was frightening in its single-mindedness.

Brrrrrrrmmmm, brrmm-brrmm, Brrrrrrrmmmm.
All they wanted was a war. Let those who want to,
speak like politicians making extreme statements
in order to stay in the middle of the road. Their
own pronouncements would always be moderate
so that their bloodlust could always be justified.

Brrrrrrrmmmm, brrmm-brrmm, Brrrrrrrmmmm.
Their mouths were like straws, their eyes more
thirsty than the driest and most terrible of deserts.
They would not tolerate any deviation from their
norm. And me, I just wanted to lay down in the road
and let them trample me, drummers, majorettes, all.

Brrrrrrrmmmm, brrmm-brrmm, Brrrrrrrmmmm.
And then I saw my swan flying low into the west.
If we could just go together that would be best,
I thought, but as its not possible and as I have lost
everyone who matters to me, I will let them trample
me till we all realise people matter more than beliefs.

Brrrrrrrmmmm, brrmm-brrmm, Brrrrrrrmmmm.
But astonishingly they knew it already. The procession
parted around me to protect me from harm, and my
passions and conceits were put into proper perspective –
as my own. One of them helped me up, hoping
I was alright. We were all laughing together at the end.

Scarecrow
1.

Mistress of these BSE-manured fields, I look out
upon my precisely realised furrows
with delight; my beautiful birds are ravens
and albatrosses – no common or garden
 crows and gannets for a queen of my majesty –
which wheel and cry
in the angry unfeeling sky
before settling in serried ranks around me
to stare balefully at you
like they did in that Hitchcock film.

And you all avert your eyes hysterically
disbelieving that I, a silver-birch and wicker woman
dingle-dangling in my flippetty-floppetty hat
can shake my arms like this
and move my legs like that.
So you don't see me take flesh
with my long and lovely fashion model legs,
my actress breasts and my pornographic bum.

You only see my old rags flapping dolefully
across oddly angled branches and sticks
in the bitter screeching wind.
And you don't want to look
at my fabulous velvet gown (which is red.
And purple of course,
and inlaid with rare semi-precious jewels
brought for me from Madagascar
by our fine upstanding men).
No, I don't scare you at all.

And you don't see me
daintily step down from my cross
and make my way across the red carpet
of entrails my birds have kindly laid for me
over the muddy rivetted earth
towards your unconscious complacency.
You do not see me on my knees,
my gorgeous crown nestling in his pubis
as I suck your man dry
over and over again.

And afterwards when I have delicately patted
my mouth with my cloth of Flemish lace,
reapplied my lipstick and returned my
shining and by no means flippetty-floppetty crown
to its rightful place on my lovely head,
none of you know or understand
what has happened,
except vaguely; you notice that things are somehow
different, something is missing between you all
which you can't put your fingers, or anything else
on. And I, all innocent satisfied smiles,
am back in my rags, alone with my beautiful birds
on my ricketty tumbledown cross

Scarecrow
2.

I am tired of dingle-dangling,
my darling birds having taken leave
of absence
so there are no crows to scare.
It's a mercy though that at least
I can move my arms like this
and I can move my legs like that;

to find myself brushing my tresses
and trying to choose which dress
to wear for the funeral.
I only possess two black ones,
both of them little
and neither of them sombre.
Quite unsuitable.

Should one wear jewellery?
A hat and veil? I really don't know.
What *do* you wear
to your own funeral?
Certainly a hat.
I'm quite sure of that.
But I'm not so

sure I'm truly mourning
or sad to see him go.
Sometimes we were lovers, sure,
But its not as if we were ever
really friends or anything.
He was always, always on at me
to 'be myself'. Whatever that means!

I mean I ask you!
Would you want to be a scarecrow?
All awkward branches
and dead wood?
No, I don't think so.
Well, neither would I.
But why oh why am I crying?

Its making my mascara run,
which is appropriate I suppose
under the circumstances.
But not now, not before I've even
left the house, turning an elegant
if patent leather heel, as I step
into the limo behind the hearse.

You see? As ever, my priorities
have little to do with what he meant
to me and I cannot see
beyond my own appearance.
I do so wish it could have been me.
Anyway, never mind! This one will just have
to do. It'll be alright if I keep my coat on.

Scarecrow
3.

I can feel something small dingle-dangling
from the confused twigs of my hair. It is
a little spider which has inadvertently fallen
out from under my flippetty-floppetty hat
and, poor little thing, it is trying to climb back
up its tiny thread again, wanting to return to
the warmth of my safe welcoming darkness.

Thank goodness I can move my legs like this
and move my arms like that. I can help. I'll
take my hat off. There. That's right. In you get!
I think I'll take a walk now, back to the sunny
Sunday morning breakfasts I used to take with
my mother before she had the fall which turned
her face black because of the warfarin she was on

for her heart. We are sitting together sipping
our tea and eating warm croissants which she has
smothered with too much butter. She is still in
her dressing gown with peachy smears of make-up
down the collar from where she tried to cover up
the marks on her neck. I am asking her all about it
and tutt-tutting sympathetically whenever

she pauses. I am being very careful not to upset
her by telling her about how difficult it has lately
become to prevent bits of myself breaking or
falling off. She doesn't even know that I pass
my days and nights nailed to a post trying to
scare away the crows who, as ever, take not a blind
bit of notice of how I am feeling or who I am.

So I do not tell her about the silly little spider
who clings to me under my hat for help when
all about her, including bits of my very self, are
being blown away by the icy winds of reality,
buffeting the wooden bones and jumble sale
clothes of my frail sense of who I am, spreading me
willy-nilly across the fields I was built to protect.

Scarecrow
4.

Have you never seen a scarecrow running, sprinting across
winter fields, stick arms and stick legs moving like this
and like that and so fast that you would think she was a witch
with her skirts flying as dark as a manta ray's behind her?
You would never know she was shrieking dad-dad-dad-dad,
her stick feet never seeming to touch the ground as she blew
like a dead leaf in the wind across the miles of her hysteria.
You would be so distracted by her fearful fleeting that you
would not see that despite the fisting wind the sky had become
a sickly purpled grey and that great balls of fire were looming
out of it and dropping in burning dollops all across the land.
She has been running from the terror of finding she is not
who she is and she is what she is not. It is like a snake which
has made a frightened static bird of her for so many years that
now the act of flight is such a release that she starts singing
goodness-gracious-great-balls-of-fire, as her sap rises filling
her wooden whorled eyes with tears which stream down her
her face. She is dancing now not running, arms uplifted to
the thickening sky, delirious and laughing in expectation of
of a ball of fire rolling out of the clouds and dropping on her.
The desire to be burning gives her so much pleasure that she
finds herself coming sexually. And finally it looms, booms
and falls, and her dingle-dangle body of sticks, cobwebby skirt
and dirty old blouse are all consumed. Relieved at last that
she has become a pathetic heap of charcoal and fragments on
the muddy mire, she looks up and then joins a flock of crows
flying overhead, cawing triumphantly and feeling utterly free.

Scarecrow
5.

Sally Mander was a nice woman,
a little chubby, somewhat grubby, but nice.
She rose half barking from the cinders
of those dark maddened days

keeping her attention focussed
on practicalities. No fussing. No frills.
Just getting on with what was left
of the rest of her life.

You could see a certain sadness
in her slightly hooded eyes
but a warm cheerful smile
would always arise
whenever the occasion required it.

She would patiently tell you
that really everything was alright
and *really* you weren't to worry.
She had a job, a place to live, and the
serenity you only get from being yourself.

Everybody is very friendly, very kind,
she'd say, obliquely referring
to the possibility that they might not be.
I'm a little lonely, but that's nothing
new now is it? Not for me.

The only problem is my dreaming –
Whereas once I was always me
which would often terrify me
when I woke up and found I wasn't,
now I always have the same dream:

I'm a dingle-dangle scarecrow
in a flippetty-floppetty hat
and I can move my legs like this
and I can move my arms like that…

Yes I know, its silly isn't it!
I don't mind that. No, the trouble is
the crows cawing and a man with a face
like my father's who always comes
every night and sets me on fire.

But never mind me! I'm having a
wonderful time otherwise! I've made
friends with a woman across the road.
She's persuaded me to buy a Mynah bird.

childhood:

When young I used to go to church and pray
That how and who I felt myself to be
Would either make me change or go away
And then I'd be alright and I would see
Myself as others did and just the same
As they all were. Then I'd feel looked after
And exultant, believing in the game
Of life, sure of love from God the Father.
Afterwards when I got home and my own
Dad wasn't there, I'd play in Mum's wardrobe
In the dark beneath her dresses and moan
For God to bite a hole through my earlobe.
Churches were made of stone and dead people's bones.
But with my mother's things I was not alone.

adolescence:

The filigree curtains filled with hot air,
Billowing secretly, exposing me
Anxiously squeezing spots, pulling out hair
And worrying whether I'd ever see
A reflection I could live with. Fuming,
Oblivious to the increasing heat
Of my own self-importance consuming
Me, I examined my nails and feet –
As ever they were wanting. I found how
Frightened I was, and hating the nets, sucked
Them back in again, then closed the window
And slapped myself, feeling completely fucked.
Afterwards I sat and cried on my bed, glad
No-one knew self-harm had stopped me feeling sad.

Lamb

Wanting to bleat, and scrawl profanities
Across the uncontaminated dreams
Which stroked up safe feelings of sanity,
Gently touched, between my childhood screams,
I'd yearn to curse what god there was and shout
That what was done to me was never fair;
And let no so-called god of goodness doubt
That all it did was further painfully tear
My soul in two. Then I thought I *would* mind
Being wool-soft and weeping – lambed to make
A leering hungry wolf of God who'd find
Me such a sweet and tasty little cake.
No, I'd rather not do what I want to do.
 I think it's better to be quiet, don't you?

Ullysseic

Mayday. Mayday. Alpha-Bravo-Tango.
I can't remember to keep you in mind.
Sirens screeching on the rocks of my soul
Howl derisively that it's winter time.
This blossom isn't blossom. Its not snow.
Withering sadness has dashed all my hopes
Into dust and forgotten dreams. I know
Now this terrible noise means I can't cope
With who I am without your love; which seems
So hard to believe in, even when you're there
In my face shouting that you have always been
Constant, even as I careered god-knows-where.
When I won't listen with my wide open ears,
You are the rope which binds me. I must not fear.

Grandiose x 2.

1.

"Father, we forgive You that you know not
What You do. We understand our reward
Shall be in heaven and we say: so what
If in the meantime we have to be taught
What it means to suffer and then to die.
We are as resilient as your beard
Is long, and we can always laugh or cry
When its gets to be worse than we feared.
We have all the resources that we need
Between us. And You're envious, You know,
Because we are able freely to feed
Each other love, while we reap what we sow.
So you may dig your infantile vengeance mine.
But we've got the gold. We've had it all the time."

2.

And ye-es, You may be forgivable,
Just about, because it's true You suffer too –
All power, dread beauty and visible
Lack of human feeling. You have no clue,
Well not much, to put us all through this mill.
It's just as well You are semi-detached.
Although it's curiously strange that still
Your high omnipotence cannot be matched
By equivalent emotional sense.
But then again that's what *we* are here for,
To have it for You – for omniscience
To be genuine it must have a flaw.
Seeking Your reflection isn't vanity.
Not when You're split and spliced to humanity.

Anabiosis

Whilst in epi-spasm an inner voice, usually dumb, says:

"You know perfectly well how things are
And how they should be
And how they could be
Are all part of the 360 degree
Spectrum of action's possibilities.

That does not stop you from feeling helpless,
I know, but to claim
'insight makes no difference',
Though it may be true, is lazy, feckless,
'Something must be done'.
That's what people say.

This then is that something that must be done:

Dwell in the flameless glow between head and heart
Always look again at others, let them see who you are.
Give everything of yourself to everything you do.
Hurt no-one in going where you will.
Take your own advice.
Hear what others are feeling

And then there's the sick bag.
It's for when you fail,
When you are selfish and manipulative
Or hiding beneath how others want to see you.
It's for crawling into and crying
If you care to give a toss.

Now return to what you know
Between these poles
And carry on
As if you don't need to know about either
Because in yourself you know, you know,
How to be and what to do."

But, in spasm I'm usually deaf and can't hear a thing.

The voice replies, "Don't lie. You know, you know."

Wash Cycle.

The washing machine, like a boxer, was so purposeful
With its cheerful repetitive droning
Sounding fit and easy and promising to be
As powerful and strong as you could wish for
Set on its 'gentle' wash cycle.
I am full of hope and expectation.

Why then are the towels so rough,
Underwear as hard as last year's first full frost,
And the crinkles in all my clothes
As multifariously sharp and higgled as
All the knives in my drawers?
I don't mean to whinge but it feels unfair somehow.

Why are the sheets tossed like frozen seas?
My ship-shaped iron is hotter than hell
But struggles to impose desired horizontality
On crunched up creases despite repeated pressing
On the steamer to help it plough on through.
What would people think of someone in hard clothes?

They would still be clean.
It wouldn't be as if they were dirty or anything.
Underneath I would be clean
And in my heart despite my thoughts
I am not really a dirty person at all.
I'll wear them as they are; and see who my friends are.

But it's the towels which bother me most.
Crisped staccato, as comforting as lies,
Yet wet and welcome as bad dreams in a cold bath.
What is the *point*? I saw the drowned in Bangladesh
On the TV floating amongst their towels
And I thought of holiday makers by the pool

I couldn't understand the human condition
Essentially marooned in juxtapositions and oxymorons.
I didn't know why I'd want to either, but I did
And I do and I know there is no point.
Unless, that is, that dirtying and washing clothes
Stitches our truths in time which tell us it all matters anyway!

Dream

Every edge
Was outlined in red,
The whole a golden glow.

Too, the pure
Glamour of truth was
Anyway a lure from the lie I lived.

So I picked
Up my skirts
And tripped from the hurt

Holding my heels
In my hands
Serene and wanting to walz

Away with
The wonder of being
Free to wander where I would

On the arm
Of my majestic God whose
Curious consort I had always been;

Secure in my delusion
Completely proud I could
Always assuage his awful priapism,

Nurture our children
Sure they'd better nurture
Theirs and they theirs and so on.

Ah me, how sad
I was that truth is a noose
Ensuring I would know otherwise.

Already the ancient Greeks
And the modern Hindus knew
With their lusty bodies and high camp

Statuary, I was so very
Wrong – the ache in my god's
Tired phallus could never be soothed,

People can never
Be perfected yet remain
As they are, weak and wonderful

At one and
The same time. Our
Human condition couldn't stand it!

We'd have to find some
Way to mind whichever way
An other parallel world may be shaped.

Meanwhile this one's a joy
With its vulnerabilities made flesh,
Its dreams as diffuse and insubstantial

As hell
With its dreadful losses
And its random lack of fairness,

Yet somehow perfect
With its exquisite oxymorons
And its deep understanding of love.

This one's what we've got
To make of what we will until and
Ever after we've allowed ourselves to love:

Love alone is the only thing
Which renders all wretchedness
Minute, makes every life have meaning.

That's what wraps my vision
In crimson and gold, its lustre
A snook at the all and one source of sadness.

!!!

Bear

I love my family
I love my home
I am full of love for humankind
(But I cannot bear myself).

I am moved by love
I am moved by loving
I love it that most people are nice
(I cannot bear myself).

I can move the stuckness of others
I'm able to give them hope
They're always so kind, grateful.
(I cannot bear myself).

Last night I dreamed my baby
Could breathe underwater
And when she lifted her head
Above the surface, she still could!

She dove forward towards me
Forming a beak, a mandarin
Goose able both to swim
And to fly, and to breathe

Anywhere! She passed
Behind me and I forgot her
As I got and get on with agapeic
Care for others who mainly

Were grateful. When I woke
With an ursine growl at who
I was again I knew my job
Is simply to bear myself.

My big bearded hands
My huge hairy coat
My snorter of a snout
And my wordless gruntings

All have to be borne
Till I've finally gone.
Only then will you know
Who I am, I'm afraid.

Shame

Shame draws us towards the charismatic chandelier
Shafting spectra pointedly in all directions,
Lighting up all the truth and all the lies with equal clarity
So that it becomes impossible to know
Which is which and what is what.
(And I squirm, new-born, naked and small, Mother.)
But this is no relativist rant about subjectivity.
It is a description of Creation's shame
That despite encompassing all and everything
The poor Thing cannot in and of itself decide
To take a moral position about anything.
(And I bunch up my little face and hands and squall, Mother.)
Too grand and all-encompassing to care
It leaves that to mothers of babies
To herders of sheep, to builders of houses,
To washers of clothes, to criminals, cripples and children, to the
Great majority who happen mainly to be nice.
(And I long for you to heed my call, Mother.)
It leaves it to us, in other words, to you and to me.
And our job is to try and colour what we get
With reason and rhyme, to understand what we live through.
To fail to do so and ignore Fate's unkindnesses, to be uncaring
Is to be grandiose, as impartial as immortality itself,
(And my need for your succour is my only, my all, Mother.)
As it courses through evolution in genomic sequences
Sometimes available in discreet packets to some of us
Limited-time-serving mortals. Sometimes. But to most us – never.
The gnosis of self-effacing scientists, religious historians,
Road sweepers and dinner ladies helps, but, still, there's no excuse
(Your neglect is unbearable, I'm heading for a fall, Mother.)
For failing to care. Not to care is to commit wrong knowingly.
So how do we avoid doing that? What do we have to do?
Well, we know what we feel we mustn't do.
Though what we feel we mustn't, may be what we must
Calling us to that corner of our lives which we want to ignore,
(And my frightened scream, then somehow stalls, Mother.)
Pulls us there, make us look at that which is unclear
And at what we fear, leaves us gasping for certainty,
Petrified beneath poisoned blankets of despair
Which smother all hope yet light up truth and lies with the colours
Of all possible meanings in all possible hues
(And my mind is my body knowing love is all, Mother.)
And parabolas of parallel worlds in all possible permutations
Of everything placed before us, ensuring we know neither
What to do or how to be. Which is actually wonderful! We have to
Find out! Choose morally, risk our choices may be full of error,
But knowing that love and caring alone can be our guide.

Rain

Under our umbrellas the truth
Lies. Invisible for not being rained
Upon by the exigencies of affect,

So pristine it can be paradigmed
Ad infinitum by the wise-worded
Intellectuals who can infer

Anything from anything. I am
Out in the rain, as stupid as fuck,
Yet somehow peculiarly lucky

And wet. I knew I was wet not wise
From an early age, envying the girls
For their communion dresses and

Their perfect sugar-spiced pigtails;
Grovelling to grown-ups with my
Perfect slug and snail-clean fingernails

And my fear of persecution.
A lifetime in the rain ever since
Has left me oxymoronic,

Cynical but ecstatically purposed
To try and make the world
A better place for others.

For me, death cannot come
Soon enough, although I am told
I may be lying to myself.

Well, no 'maybe' about it.
The truth is I know where I stand
(lie) in the world of water

And I know it comes from the sky.
So when I look up and wonder why
I feel so terribly empty inside

Drowning in anxiety and maudlin
Feelings of love and fear
Wailing and crying, 'Oh dear, Oh dear,'

The wet world of affect and lies
Reassures me still that the truth
Has been well worth avoiding.

And time, in hurricane or humidity
Snow melt, storm, flood, fog or mist
Washes and wafts me under its spell,

Makes fish food of me or grains of sand
Or the shapes and shadows in the clouds –
Anything!!! But always absolutely alive.

The Point

It seems no amount of words
Advice, therapy, friendship or love
Will ever make someone sensible out of me.

It seems I don't know how to link
Thoughts and feelings together calmly
Certain that what I think and feel are one

It seems that the me that I am
Must always be uncertain of myself
And actually ambivalent about everything

It seems insight into that is no cure
That I may change structurally with age
But the personality flaws are with me to the end

It seems there is no point to me at all
That any meaning to who and what I am
Can only be found in my interactions with others

It seems then that I must retreat from that
In order to check out the seeming and find out
If appearances are deceptive or express what's within.

It seems I must become a hermit
Find the truth in the winds of isolation
As it has been unobtainable in relationships

It seems truth is somehow so important
And not to be found anywhere except inside
My contradictory thoughts and frightening feelings

It seems that if I try to find it through others
I will only get more and more lost which is okay
But it is better to do it wilfully, out of choice in the end

It seems if you feel you've chosen your life
Then you meet yourself when you find you got it wrong
And apparently that is a good thing because you learn who you are

It seems that that is then all there is to it
Your job is done you can finally stop the search,
You've met your true self doppelganger whoever s/he may be

It seems you may as well let go altogether,
Wander the streets and on out into the country
Until you find you have merged with the infinite

It seems that your body, numbered but unnamed
In some mortuary drawer somewhere, will tell the story
Of your search in all its mournful glory as it lies there lumpen.

Cairns Clery

The Stillness of Flowers

Shape-scented colours cluster
Like the final few days waiting
For the waters to break for a baby.
Shored-up, pooling, huge. Silent
As the sound of everything.

Warm care-taking curves
Protect the colours of words:
Azure sepals, violet petals, rose, cerise;
As if around a deep lake in a glade
Black as the ace of spades

Where the dark rest of shade
Turns with the summer sun, caressing
Without touching, murmuring without sound,
Stiller than stasis, absolute motionlessness –
We call for pollination please

By dreaming alone of everything
In the company of loneliness. We're flowers.
And all that movement inside our sleep
Cushions the reality we will have to waken to
When day's rush and buzz

Will distract us further from
From the focus within.
Scent-shaped babies, calling for
Perfect poise in our vulnerability
We look at each other, our leaves seeking

Light nourishment, milk-and-honey rain,
Root-sucking, reflecting, transforming radiance
Into every hue in the spectrum.
Bees alight, but make no fuss
As they take up our sweetness.

In return, in hushed abandon we are the movement
Into vision of softness and colour.
Dresses of every kind and age cover
Our composure as seen and probed
We cluster in our scent-shaped colours,

Then happy to go to seed, we bend in the breezes
Of autumn and embrace death-as-part-of-life
And smile serenely to ourselves
That we are how we are regardless
Of whether or not you can see us!

Time and the Periwinkle

Do we run into hope? Or is it accidental and actually we are made, collectively, to run to it deluded we have choice? Is the search for light just an excuse for peering through the gloom and stretching a point?

Nobody can see the deep dark green hearts of the leaves following their leaders plunging and jungling into chaos; just notice it after the event – a panoply of self-absorbed circumventions.

Not unless they slow below the speed of silence, letting its utterness suspend disbelief

So that nothing that cannot be heard is joined in the cacophony of inversion called Noiselessness.

They could, if they wished, surrender, shrivel and die. Nobody would mind because

Simple vegetable surgings and occasional cyan blue petalings are neither here nor there in the great scheme of things.

Not the soft sluggish sightless ones, nor the toxic toadying uglies, or the legless earth

Eaters (so often sliced by spades my slowly dying gardening friend finds that he cries); nor too the tearful tenderers of dead wood with their rattling wings

Would know this, so busy are they simply being themselves. But high above

Dead trees do still shriek, reach for a future that's beyond them, and louder than they

Ever did while alive. All that pointless pointing in every direction

But absolutely lost in all direction and directions. No wonder they clothe their

Nakedness in leaves. Rooted to react to the earth, to ignoring the wind

And gauging temperature and barometric pressure,

To braving elemental heat and light, darkness and cold; to remembering

In trunked rings what it feels like to be still, and other such temporal irrelevancies

(rot, fungus, moth, woodworm and all – they all need to live too).

Nor I, the Dogsbane, streaking silently along at ground level, as furtive as Neurological disease through the flaked skin of history down below. But I am Satisfied getting entangled and being unwilling to be free even if I wanted to be.

Which I do. And don't. (Welcome to my world!). Here in the undergrowth we do

Distinguish between truth and lie. But only in order not to do so –

To fuse them in a wonderful mutual dependency. ('I and I').

Does the dog want to piss on me? Or will I infect his stream as he soaks me, withal

To banish him from ever doing so again? This is just one of my dour little

Oxymorons down here in the dark.

To yearn for light one must be in the dark – There's none so blind as those who cannot see, they say – And I cannot see a thing. Truly. For some reason I am always looking. 'Where?' 'Where?' I cry, always too busy not seeing to ever truly look.

I peer madly in every direction directionless. I address the problem and look at the Maps which all my life have shown me HRT and a dress is truly and really the only way out back into myself, but then I always seem to find a reason why it isn't. As if the truth would be a lie. The lie a truth. Which it is already is when you are a periwinkle (as I have already explained). So,

'Why bother?' and 'What's the point?' are the stupidest of questions. You can endure Lifetimes asking them until eventually you get this:

The truth can lie too and this proseom is not truly a lie. You are that which you are not.

And you are not what you are (And you are not who you are either, of course!).

So please don't pretend for any other reason than the sheer hell of it

That you are anything more or other than yourself. That's the Alpha and Omega.

But the real miracle is that dead or alive we somehow contrive to make that matter.

It is our consternation and our joy that our insignificance is as wide as all the skies

PATIENTS' PATIENCE

My sadness seeps in silence
Like melting ice secretly

Becoming water below its
White horizontal perfection.

Gritting their eyes with glitter:
I smile, soothe and understand,

Shining, radiant; reflecting
Everything fine in them,

That blind they cannot see
For themselves without me.

They think I'm moon-like,
Love how I seem to feel

And know who they are,
Imagine I have no cracks

Must be a hallowed one,
Must know who I am.

But beneath my brightness
I am flowing into the sea

With such quiet relentlessness
You would fall right through

If you stepped on my floe,
Find yourself drowning

In all the subaquan torrents
Streaming from my heart

Whilst I appeared perfect
A round polar-white plate

Of responsiveness above my
Blood-red seeping blood

THE PUDDLE AND THE GATES

The birth and death gates
Are heavier and older than the earth,
Bigger than the sky…

I have only seen one easy
Death in all the length of my life,
and just one easy birth…

Why, then, must landing on
And leaving this earth be so very
Hard, such a trial,

I'll never know. I do know that!
But I think I may have learned too
It helps a little to smile.

Not at the horror or the hell
Or even at the brief heavenly moments
Which help define them,

But at the existential duty that
We have to find some kind of
Meaning in the times of our lives.

(And not just any meaning –
It has to feel as true as trees are tall
Or small, and just as complex).

So It helps to sleep,
To go to the moon, For some milky
Mother-still perspective,

Effectively distance ourselves from
From time to time, even every night
From the pain of Estrangement,

Reconnect with synchrony, with
All time in concert, happening now
At this moment in these words,

The children we were, the people we
Are now, and the sediment we will one
Day become at the bottom of the pond

In stillness, in sleep. Now. (But
Maybe not in dreams. I'm not sure,
They're sometimes so fierce).

The puddle is still, its shape
Reflecting the moon, inviting
Us to look up and down,

See how temporary everything is,
How time is as long as we make it
And as short; and everything

We are between the gates, as we
Swim like tadpoles or whales
From shore to shore

Making waves, making ripples,
Or nothing at all, just as we please,
Matters only as much as we care.

And the puddle and the gates,
If you look at them from the moon
Are beautiful and poignant, sure.

But the mote in the eye of creation,
The truth which belies the cold
Collective indifference of Space

And subtly subverts its iciness,
Is the comfort of a cup of tea
Or a loved one's smile –

That same smile between us all.
The whole thing turns upon this -
What is truly timeless

Isn't so much the struggle through
the Gates of birth and death, nor the
Primordial or post-modern puddle

In which we swim. It really is the
Taking and giving of kindness
Through all the lengths of our lives.

Searching for a Home

Context

In 1642 Civil war was breaking out across England, mainly driven by different understandings of Christianity and ten years of famine. Lionel Cranfield, Earl of Middlesex, lived in Forthampton near Tewkesbury on the edge of the Gloucestershire/Worcestershire border through which the river Severn (Habren) passes. For years he had been jealously guarding his herd of captive deer which he kept at nearby Corse Lawn. Anyone who tried to steal one was summarily executed. Eight years previously his Keeper of the Deer, a man named John Beale, had been murdered by poachers. Cranfield had had them hung. The massacre of the deer at Corse Lawn with which this story begins was a joint venture between local gentry and peasants. Having killed the deer they did not eat them, but left them on the ground to rot. This epos starts with that incident.

List of Characters and places

Kate Beale.	Aged fourteen, John Beale's daughter.
Sophie Beale.	Aged five months, her half sister.
Rose Beale.	Their mother, widow of John Beale (ghost).
Elizabeth Raseil.	A widow.
The Marrow Boy.	'Paul' Bier, aged about fourteen, undertaker's son.
The Laz-boy.	(Laz=Lazarus), Cranfield's bastard son, Gervase (12).
Habren.	The river Severn.
The Bore.	A tidal wave which sweeps upstream.
Noadu.	The god of the wave who rides on a seahorse.
The white deer.	Only survivor of the massacre of the herd.
Brilliana Reekes	Aged nine, orphan.
Isabel Reekes	Her twin sister.
King Hu	Mythic Welsh Monarch who slays monsters
Anwyn	Hill of Souls (Glastonbury Tor)
'Pure' John Apney	Glastonbury man
Ann Apney	His brother's wife
Robert 'Greybeard'	Glastonbury 'Clubman'
Ruth 'Fine Lady'	Banbury woman
Sam and Jenny	Very young children (orphans)
Naseby	Site of the decisive battle of the English civil war
Flat Holm	Island in the Bristol Channel
The Levels	Peat bogs/Marsh land in Somerset
St Mary the Virgin	Church in Putney
The Thames	River

Also referred to:

Oliver Cromwell, Thomas Fairfax, Sir Philip Skippon and Henry Ireton, Parliamentary Generals at Naseby; Lionel Cranfield, Earl of Middlesex; Mathew Hopkins, Witchfinder General; Afanc, Crocodilian Monster; Francine Shapiro, trauma therapist; Levellers, proponents of egalitarianism.

Engenderings

SEARCHING FOR A HOME

1.

In the stilled and moist autumnal distance the slow roiling roar
Of the great river's stately swollen wave, the mighty Habren Bore,
Crashes through the purpled quiet of the dawn conscientiously.

And six hundred Deer with twelve hundred eyes are ghosted as one.
On twenty four hundred legs they look anxiously at their young;
Tensed to leap to and from the shadows of the sunrise; till they see

Seven sleek swans with necks thrust flat-forward in orange-beaked fright
Fleeing in rhythmic formation, flapping like rowers in flight
Desperately steering for the safety of Anywhere-But-Here.

The placid herd below does not tremble, knowing the roar will pass.
The deep rumble of its thunder-drone makes the munching of grass
In the gentle soak of the morning dew somehow free of fear.

Some still sleep, steam hardly rising from their nostrils and their flanks.
They've been happy all night among the shrubs; their bearing gives thanks
For the vegetative, gardened peace of this place, its tastes and scents.

Nuzzling the last of the sweet new grass, fawns, eating their breakfasts,
Trot back to their dams now and again, little tails like soft masts
Wiggling in delight, feeding forever like life is heaven-sent

2.

In a tox-ring round them collected resentment concentrates,
Silently stalking from all quarters, focused and brimful of hate.
Set on psychopathy, indifferent to the smell of bacon

And laundry washed in lavender wafting through the rose bushes. Their
Overwhelming lust to feast first and gorge on game blood and prayers
Means the steward-keeper's house has no interest they'll now take on.

His Corse Lawn home has mugs and breakfast plates broken on the floor.
And a baby's been dropped, screaming by the splintered kitchen door.
And if you find you are shocked she can be left like the deer to die

You're right, but revenge is a mirror which helps them feel confirmed
In belief Cranfield's meanness is complete – innate *and* learned.
So their teeth can be as sharp as it's been deep… Deer deaths multiply.

Their killers lay with them, love them as they slay them, try to eat
Their innocent, bleeding hearts and their sweetly-turned other cheeks
In an orgy of uneasy dispassionateness, frenzied anxiety and greed,

Managing to merge immersion in action in the present
With dissolution of all human kindness. Yet they do sense,
Still, the unfairness of revenge on mere kept deer – there was no need.

3.

In the woods, Kate, truffle-hunting for John Beale's wife, Corse cook,
And her own mother, watches everything. Hidden in a tree she looks
And sees the leather and felt-booted avengers a breath away.

Then, above the din of the deer writhing raw on the lawn, from the house
She hears her baby sister's mewls. Frightened, moving like a mouse,
Innocuous and as invisible as the air of the day,

And deep-worried where their mother is, Kate scoops up her sister,
Sophie, then scurries up the stairs, tries to deny the sick vista
Which now envelops her mind, mirroring the monstrousness outside.

Reaching the small bay turret on the roof she sees her mother
Angst-hover in the air, her feet on fire, dead. Yet another
Sad ghost. This ghastly morning can be borne no more. Her sore-numbed eyes

Wide, Katie, feeling her heart fear-thumping, peers down at the lawn.
Smelling and hearing the carnage below, her vision is torn -
For want of a lesser evil twixt that and Mam's fiery spectre.

Preferring the life in her little sister's soft warm smile,
She fuss-fiddles with her frock, whispers the deer *will* revive while
The door and windows *will* self-repair; says she'll always protect her.

4.

If Forthampton could be razed as if it wasn't ever there
Then neither would these offal-tasters here be. All would be fair.
So the great stag, who alone escaped, thinks, plumps for extreme measures

To deal with this dire submission to death of does, fawns
Flapping like moths in the sun on this sumptuous manicured lawn.
Let this serf's home be Forthampton – he will destroy it for pleasure.

The door, his imagined French Windows, wide open, in he trots.
He's all berserked, passing Middlesex's ornamental pots
And family paintings ascending the anodyne, airless stairs,

And in passing hooks a star-bright white nightgown on his antlers
Inadvertently. Not blindness, nor 'hearing' Cranfield's banter
Can stop him reaching that baleful balcony open to the air.

The children don't see him in Corse, (or Forthampton), towering,
Chill-stilled by the butchered forms which lie below. He's glowering,
Watching too as hate turns to sate on the lawn where nothing is good.

But these men below have devoured nothing! Only their pinch-pursed
Brows and soaking-wet red clothes truth-speak of the obscene and cursed
Furrow they really did plough. Shame-faced, they melt back into the woods.

Engenderings

5.

Kate shudders, can't look at her mother burning any more. Nor
Down at the still heaving meat on the grass. What exactly for?
If she can not think that it is pointless, she knows what she fears.

Behind her the stag senses her despair and shares it. The baby
Seems oblivious, yet all-knowing. Her smile's safe. No 'maybe'
About her contentment – she's in her sister's arms with a deer!

Kate finds a fugue state soothing her. Thinking it must be Father
Sophie sees above her, she leans on him so he can gather
Them in his arms, wrap them in their mother's fine white, linen nightgown.

'Mammy's a ghost on fire, Dad,' she says. 'Look, there in the air.'
She points through the gown hanging twixt his horns and her birds-nest hair.
Neither can stop her seeing Rose Beale's shade is now gone, fallen down

Like the life from the carcasses below. And her dad's a *stag*!?
'Where shall we live, Daddy, now Mam's gone and can not cook? Our bags
Must be packed and we must surely go now? Live elsewhere, not too far?'

Facing him, she wraps the gown smelling of Mam and tarragon
Round her sister and herself. Her broken heart has a new song
Of acceptance now; tiny, yes, but real as the farthest star.

6.

The darkness in the stag's eyes goes out like a light as he stares.
He would neither leap from this balcony nor trample these bairns,
Senses the innocence, like animals', of Sophie and Kate.

As those who've murdered the herd may too have once meant not to kill.
They were hungry for years, but resisted revenge until
Their seethe-waters broke, surprising them with the power of their hate

As vicious as an infant's stark, violent need. Restorative
Natural justice evolved ten years before authoritative
Cant and rationales would be used to close the doors of history

On Gloucestershire's famine, so infanticidal, so profound
That at bare wooden tables and empty kitchens all around
The county, for far too many people food was a mystery.

So they who marched on Corse and massacred the deer on the lawn
Did so with all hope and all due empathy for others shorn,
Swept aside like lice-ridden locks on the sad whore of civil war.

The stag starts to cry, great guilt-dark tears of remorse for never
Leading the herd away and not knowing he had to sever
All connection, with all the people, all across the country, sure.

7.

What, if he could, would he do to them? Kate wonders, unafraid
Now, not just of him but of all the horrible men who made
Meat of his herd. Death stench rises with their souls, sizing her fear.

She would touch his tears and those of her mother's ghost if only
She wasn't gone, consumed by the fire. She might feel too lonely
If he was not here. Crying herself, she tap-touch dries his tears.

Sophie's aglow, radiant. But Kate can't wet-nurse her, her breasts
Are still little. And all the adults are gone. It would be best
To find a goat or a cow, but Mam said they'd all left for slaughter

Weeks ago. The stag's warm breath smells of forests green and meadows
Pure. For all she knows her mother may be dead 'neath a hedgerow.
'Our mammy's dead,' she says, seeing if this truth sounds like it ought to,

Hearing how she sees it, choked and broken, sounding like a plate,
Sophie starts to cry too. Kate, cracked, says, 'we must leave and go straight
To Wells where our Auntie Jane lives, ask her for some food and some room.

It may be miles away, I don't know, nor just where it may lie
But if the stag could take us then I'm certain we will not die!
But how to help the hart downstairs? If we don't he'll trap-perish soon.'

8.

'Pull him by the tail, you silly goose,' her mother's fond voice sighs.
From the garden below! For a moment, the truth's sore belied –
Mam alive! Kate's confused; was not Mam in flames which still crackled

A moment ago? She peeps through the battlements, Mam's nightgown
At her nose, after laying Sophie carefully down. The sound
Of their mam's voice has reassured them both even though it cackled.

'Where are you, Mam?' Keeping her eyes off the awful shit-red pile
She peers at shadows in every tree, every bush and shrub while
Behind her the hart bit-champs, hoof-clatter ringing like flattened bells.

She peers everywhere but cannot see her. 'Please, Mam, where are you?'
'Leave Sophie there,' comes reply. 'Get her after. Now pull his tail, do!
Because you can't stay there, my silly goose! Or you'll join me in hell.'

She sees an old woman twice Mam's age in rags atop the mound.
It cannot be – she's ancient, bent, a crone, 'waving not drowned',
Queen of Carrion enthroned on dead meat. Kate catches her breath.

'Mam, you're so old!?' But her mother can't hear her above the chunder
Of the great stag's frenzied hooves hitting the stone floor like thunder.
Kate fears he could leap right over her head and plunge down to his death.

9.

And Sophie is screaming. Kate must be brave, calm him down again.
She stays before him, hushing him; reaches up, cling-hugs his mane
And hanging onto his neck soft-speaks love until he's soothed, at peace.

Then she explains that she will be helping him backwards down the stairs
And all will be well, which he knows, doesn't he, because *she* will be there!
Speaking with certainty, she might be her mam! Like her, at least.

Not like that crone-mother, a sick witch from her own fevered mind,
Surely, please, not still there? Letting go she looks down again, finds,
Feeling faint, Mam in all her ages everywhere now, pullulate:

A young lady in muslin gliding through the roses with her cuttings; a fine
Corpse, white as snow, on the steps; an apron-clad plump woman with wine
In the herb garden; a girl not much older than Kate herself by the gate.

And all of them Rose Beale and every one more real than any dream
That Katie has or had or will have all her life's length. To scream
Can't be considered, 'cos both stag and baby are tranquil now, still.

'I am imagining her everywhere! Magic of a witch –
It must be. She can't be everywhere. I'm going mad, must stitch
My mind's figments together into one truth – and do as she wills.'

10.

With so many 'mothers' in Corse Lawn and all of them hers, Kate
Lets Mam's voice alone be true, and now she knows, if rather late,
The stag is not her dad, she squeezes past him to the stairs and pulls.

And pulls. Made angry, he could kick her down the stairs. His alarm
Cuts the morning, echoes through all mornings, calls cervids to arms
Against what has gone and what will come. Their revenge must be full.

Not comprehending, Katie holds tight to his taut little tail
With one small hand; clutches the door frame with the other. To fail
Is not on offer, but he's three times her size, thirty times stronger.

She tugs like ten thousand girls with multitudes of mothers, but
The stag stays fast, moves not forward nor backwards, is sadly stuck.
She must go with Sophie, leave him to die. She has strength no longer.

Not knowing what she says or who she is, she just makes murmur
If he's not her dad he may one day be her husband. Firmer
Intuitions have not before borne fruit, but she's sure he'll survive.

Going back down the stairs with Sophie, her arms feel like branches.
The great stag's hooves gallop above, raining thunder in tranches
Of huge, lightening-shocked madness. The whole house rocks. Cracks start to
thrive,

11.

Latticing the walls. Her stick legs, feeling heavy, huge as trees,
Take each step down like it's her last, for fear she'll tumble like scree
And then be part of the detritus at the bottom of the stairs.

But, madly, she feels strong as the trees, could dash the whole house down
With her wooden arms, kick-smash it with her lumber legs. Her crown
Of vine and leaf would proclaim her Viridiana the Fair.

Green in tooth and claw, with a vegetable brain. And whether
By sudden rage or slow strangling, she'd raze her home. Together
With Sophie, forget it, go, find sanctuary wherever

It is that her auntie lives in Wells. But she's getting knotted
Now, becoming gnarled, green with sick and forgetting just what it
Is she's doing here, now from reality she's been untethered.

Each stair feels like a year to get down. She knows she must not drop
Her sister. She feels so sick and her head is a spinning top,
Knows she's un-becoming. Above, the trapped stag's still thunder-running.

The house crumbles; plaster, paintings tumble – unwanted discards,
Leaves in autumn, Kate thinks. Then her brain unscrambles 'cos it's hard
To feel fibrous as wood when your sister's safety asks for cunning

12.

And you know the house will crush you if you do not leave it now.
So defy your lignification, Kate, move like the sleek prow
Of some sea vessel, cut through this broken house on suck-dried marsh land.

T'will be rebuilt in Queen Anne's time and 'lovingly refurbished'
As a hotel anyway in three centuries. Sophie's wish
Will be done, whatever. Her will is to survive. Please understand,

Green and ghastly as you are, you must go, seek solace in hope.
It would deliver dreams of undoing all this, help you cope
With being bereaved and provide promise of belonging afresh

In a new home with your mammy's fat sister suckling Sophie,
Comforting you with soft words, and cuffing Cousin Joe's jokey
References to your homeless need for an orphanage-with-crèche

As she makes you remember again what it's like to feel safe.
That's right! Go to the kitchen, wrap up some of your mam's sweet cake
And run! Before the stag has brought this house crashing down on Corse Lawn.

For he's freeing himself with his mad, thundering still-running
Now, but could take you to Wells if you've the luck and the cunning
To repair and make good his terrible loss and help him to mourn.

13.

Dreading all her mothers and the dead deer on the grass, Kate hastens down
To the kitchen, takes beer and cake. The house, like snow, falls around
Her, each flake harder than the bricks and plaster of which it is made

Because she knows this is the last time she'll ever see her home.
But also 'cos she'd like to have died too if she'd been on her own,
To be again with Mam. But memories of her must fade!

Greener now than any forest shade and faster than the light,
Kate bundles the food and scoops up her sister who shows no fright,
Grief-runs out the front door as her home quakes to rubble behind her,

Then she's rendered stone-still, beholding carrion crows and rooks
Atop the red, grue-black pile. The sight of her dead mother hooked
By her stays to the corner of the steps, her eyes pecked, doth blind her

Only a moment before she turns back to see the great stag
Standing midst the rising dust where once her house stood, like a flag
Of continuity between what once was and what once will be.

Shining through the debris of her home the dazzling morning sun
Lightens the hart and turns him white but she knows he will not shun
Them, though his hurt, shock and sadness mean that still he will never be.

14.

But his heart's grown and with it his stature. He too turns his back,
Lets Kate place Mam's nightgown as a halter to lead them, make tracks
From this horror, across the Habren Valley, down to the famous Wells

Where great fountains of truth and wheeling arches of transcendence
In high serried ranks, hide humbly behind saints and gargoyles, fenced
In stone from famine, disease and war, and ringing with great bells!

At least that's what Mam once said when talking about Auntie Jane.
'It's lovely there, all peace and light, impossibly high. Insane
Are they who would not find succour there and safety too, like heaven,

It is, on earth!' So Kate pulls the great stag's head down and in his ear
Whispers 'we must go south and west my mammy said, and show no fear.
You're all white and I am green, but Sophie, being small, will leaven

The bloodlust of the hunters and the worries of the frightened.
They will not hurt us, I'm sure! At Wells our souls will be lightened
Because Sophie and I will be safe again and you'll feel forgiven.'

She scrambles through the rubble and finds another shawl to wrap
Around his middle and fastens Sophie safely to his back.
Never having heard of Lot's wife they leave, hoping to be shriven.

15.

But there can be no sweet comfort, no joy, in being bereaved
All they know is that they must go on till their lives are seized
Too. And in the meantime cock snooks at God's mercilessness on earth,

And head for Hartpury in hope that having heard of it, she
Will find her way there and its villagers will not scream or flee
When they see them, won't believe that of goodness there is a dearth

When babies can be tied to the backs of harts and girls made green.
Through the woods now, gold and red fall-carpets of leaves make it seem,
As the sun streams down, that what happened could never have been somehow.

Sensible birds and robin-red squirrels make ready for change.
Autumn is everywhere. It's far and wide they will have to range
If they do not prepare for the trials ahead. But they're singing now

Playing too, as if there is no tomorrow, no wintertime.
And if they had no memory, Katie and the Stag would find
Right now, here in the glorious Gloucestershire woods, that all is well.

There is no past haunting here to make it contaminate or vile.
The forest is natural, there's no reason to worry while
The fecund scent of sod, leaf, moss and mould is all that they can smell.

16.

Sophie wakens, stare-watching the fall; undersides of twigs and leaves
Gently detach in the dappling. Kate listens as she breathes:
Little baby hunger sounds begin to well up. She will cry soon.

Kate suggests to the stag that they need not stop – she will dip beer
Onto Sophie's lips that she can sip some goodness, maybe hear
Their mother in her dreams when she sleeps again. It would be a boon,

If on the back of the stag she could still perhaps find comfort
Not knowing yet that she has lost their mam and truly no sort
Of mothering may ever be hers now after all that's been done.

The rhythm of the stag's haunches sets her sister back to sleep.
Now know this, which Kate does not: her sister is 'God', the 'Void', the 'Deep'
Who must forget she knows all will be well, and has become human

So she can feel helplessness. The stag, whiter in the eve-gloom
Gets restless, needs Kate's calming; Sophie's 'anguish' resounds the doom
Of his herd to his full-feeling mind. The memory itself hurts

Like her God-awful screams. So as they come to Hartpury
Their agitation emanates like elemental fury
And the people peer from their hovels at them, anxious and alert.

17.

Just then Sophie's cries get even louder. The shawl doth slip
Tying her to the hart's back. She's caught beneath him, tries to sip
Even make nip at where his teats might be. Then he it is that screams

Louder himself than if he'd been trapped or torn upon by dogs!
Kate leans down to detach her, but Sophie's sleeping like a log
Again already, as if sated, like a little cat with cream.

Belatedly, girl and stag peer at the houses in the dark
Hoping kindness will move one to let them have a stable, park
Their weary minds and bodies down, shelter on some straw for the night.

'Go away, demons!' A deep voice booms. Wails from behind a wall
Sound mad. From behind another, women's prayers, reciting the fall,
Are heard. The village seems benighted by terror and pitiful fright.

The great stag stands up tall, antlers branching into the night sky.
He cough-bellows the scared villagers to silence that they might spy
That though he's huge and white and Kate's vegetable, they do need shelter

Like any other innocents. Without it Sophie will fail
Her breath will be stopped by the cold of the night. Then a tall, pale
Boy runs from a door at Kate and with a rotten apple pelts her.

18.

It's moonless, but by bright starlight the stag somehow lets her know
That Kate should take Sophie in her arms and ride him too. Like snow,
His lucism shines in the night. Thus they thoroughfare slowly through.

Occasional missiles like shooting stars from the hovels come.
An apple core here, a turd there. None make contact save only one,
An oak-apple-headed twig-doll lands on his antlers, makes Kate coo.

Holding Sophie snug against her, Kate looks at its red patch skirt
And matching scarf, knows no little girl would throw this on the dirt.
She's been cared for dearly, loved; but made an orphan now, and for what?

Yes, join us do, Kate thinks, glad to be reminded all's not war.
Just then the stag leaps high, an arrow piercing his thigh. Sore
Does not begin to describe the pain which makes him run, makes him stop

Only when the village is past. Kate puts Sophie on the ground
And murmuring all gentleness pulls the barb out, throws it down.
Her mother's nightgown turns red as she soft-mops his wound and he cries

Silent tears that this is how it is and how it has to be.
The pale apple-thrower has followed with a marrow. 'Sorry.'
He drops it, runs back to Hartpury. 'Please', Kate tells the stag, 'Don't die.'

19.

And he doesn't. The gash on his thigh has very quickly dried –
It's become so cold now that the speed of his flowing blood tide
Has slowed and coagulation has raced. Beside him in the murk

And watching how his eyes get softer, Kate feels she's in a trance,
As emitting for a moment, it seems, a strange luminance
The hart's antlers shine in the starlit night like silver fire-works;

The contours of his body soften too, though bigger than trees
He is for that same moment, as something fundamental's eased
In his very being. Then, restored, if smaller, he makes shiver.

'We'll have to spend the night out here,' Kate says, worried, looking down.
Sophie stares right back up at her making little hungry sounds.
'You deer are used to woods, grass and bushes, but we cannot dither

Or we'll die of cold out here. We must make a blanket of leaves
In which to keep warm. Will you sleep with us? I ask you to, please,
Because, snuggled all together, our bodies will keep the cold away.'

These last days have been mellow and dry and the nights cold and crisp.
Kate's feet sweep-gather fallen foliage. The hart assents, twists,
To settle on his uninjured side. Lying with him they sleep till day.

20.

Slurping noises wake Kate next morning. She pushes leaves aside
To let the sun in, sits up to see the white deer, brown eyes wide,
Happy and content, and gently allowing Sophie to suckle.

Birdsong is chattering. A brook is gurgling. All is well.
She yawns and stretches, notices her hands are still sick-green, tells
The doe with shining antlers that yesterday they would have buckled

If he, no, she, had not so bravely borne them with such swiftness
Out of Hartpury. 'But 'twas nice that boy despite the sickness
Of his village said, 'Sorry!', gave us a marrow. Shall we eat cake,

You and I? You can't be wet nurse and hind both and still survive
Without nourishment. I'll make fire, brush your pelage, help you thrive!'
Perhaps this doe is their mam, she thinks, returned as a deer, for their sake!

Shaking her head, the hind soft-smiles refusal of fire, lets Kate
Take the little twiggy doll, give it to Sophie who's now sate.
The female deer then arises, lets Kate wash her wound with water.

Putting her sister on the great doe's back, tied with the blood-red shawl,
Kate puts the doll in the hind's antlers for safe keeping. Like a pall,
A fog then comes down all around 'Rose Beale', Corse cook, and her daughters.

21.

If it is she. Kate would like to think so, but the doe can't speak
And sadly Kate can soon see, as they wander, that she is weak.
Her wound suppurating now it's day and warmer, despite the fog.

Through the murk she makes out autumn filleting the trees which claw
Like the upturned feet of pheasants; their gold plumage on the floor
Lying around like summer dresses torn off by some rabid god

Of seasons who likes to take his time denuding them, delights
In arboreal dishabille and naked nature. The sight
Is as melancholy as the doe slow-falling to her knees.

'Oh, Cervid-Mother, please don't expire. Without you we won't find
Our way to Wells and if we don't die too then we'll lose our minds,
Lost in these woods with no care or direction at all through the trees.'

Even as she speaks Kate knows this deer can't really be Rose Beale.
Her animal nature is soft, nurturing, but she can't feel
What Mam always knew: babies and children have always to come first.

Kate will make a poultice from toadstools, place it on the doe's wound,
Having mixed moss, marrow and her sister's tears with a stick-spoon
To liquid-pulp, she will put the rest to the hind's mouth, quench her thirst.

22.

The antlered doe doesn't despair, but knows she's as near to death
As the heart of the stars are to the absence in space of breath.
She finds a calm collectedness like a crown encircling her head.

Readying herself for life-leaving, the doe does not seem sad,
Seems to see beyond the fog to some faraway wood where bad
Things like arrows don't fly and fearful homeless waifs are not made dead.

'Don't die!' Kate cries. Then Sophie starts to howl and like a gold chain
Their voices pull the doe's awareness back to this world again.
She moans against the power of the wind that takes us all away,

And which our forbears all have flown upon, unless they still live.
'Live!' Kate shouts, mashing her poultice as quick as she can to give
It to her in time. The doe's moans, the girls' screams pierce the still, fogged day.

Then a woman's voice, like a shaft of light, stills them to silence
'Stop it, children, cry no more, it won't help! You do violence
To the morn. And more angry men will come, I give you good warning!

And none of us need that! Not again.' She is beautiful, but old
Standing beneath the copper beech across the way. 'Be bold,
Girl, and don't be stupid! You're helping that hart to live this morning?'

23.

'I am!' Kate replies. 'But she's an antlered hind now, not a hart.
Her wound is deep. It is aflame, sore with pus and for a start
I am mixing a mash to put on it. She knows the way to Wells

Where my aunt lives.' 'And you know wicca ways, unless I am wrong,'
The woman says. 'So don't be alarmed. I too have known them long.
Did your mam teach you?' She smiles, picks up Sophie from the ground. 'This dell

Is safe and you'll come to no harm here, if quiet as the trees
You can be.' Picking a sloe from a bush, she gets to her knees
Beside Kate, says, 'Squeeze this into your mash it will help the healing.'

Then coos at Sophie, rocking her. 'My name is Liz Raseil
My husband died ten years ago or more and I became ill
After, would have died too if a witch had not for me had feeling.

Grief would have murdered me. I left Forthampton mad, moved down here
Alone, my children all dead of hunger or still born. My fear
Was I'd forget him so I had a stone in church inscribed then left,

And wandered these woods around till a wild woman with green skin
Like yours found me and to her stick-hut lead me and took me in,
Nurse-taught me to heal with herbs and berries, with sickness to be deft.

24.

'Your antlered doe-mother will do alright now. I watched you make
That salve and knew from your vomitous colour that it will take
But a short time before you're both slain if you don't stay in the woods.'

Putting on the poultice, hushing the hind's moans, and murmuring
Endearments, Kate's blood has froze. This woman is wise, but stirring
Feelings of fear in her too. She knows they should run, if they just could.

'I thank you, Elizabeth Raseil, but we must move on
As soon as our pale, beautiful hind is well again; be gone
We must be, for my auntie lives far-many a long mile from here.'

'You are a clever and yet foolish girl, I see,' said the witch.
'If you are not raped you will be killed and thrown into a ditch
By soldiers hard with war, yet soft-scared of a green girl with a deer.'

She sneers. 'What is more, 'twill be winter soon and cold may kill you.
I think you should stay with me till the spring, only then will you
Be able to go all the way to Wells. Will not Tewkesbury do

Just as well?' 'No,' says Kate. 'Our aunt doesn't live there! But we'll stay
With you gladly and give you thanks till this deer welcomes the day
She's well enough to pilgrim for her people and take us there too.'

25.

'Tis expedience makes Kate consent. Sophie's hungry again
And this woman seems to know how to make remedies for pain.
But it won't be hard to bid her goodbye when the hind's recovered.

Returning Sophie to the doe's teats for some minutes, Kate then helps
The deer to her feet, must hold her up now with Mam's nightgown 'belt',
So unsteady is she. 'Don't worry, I've straw nearby and cover,

Your doe will be alright!' 'She is not mine! I think she's a queen.
Her antlers are a silver crown. A male she may once have been,
But caring for us has confirmed for her that nurturing's more true

To how she feels. We will, I thank you, follow you to your home
So grateful for your shelter while winter throws its ice-cold stones
Down across the land. Will I keep house and forage for food for you?'

'Thank you, my dear, that's all I would need and is ever so kind
Of you. I see you have a flask of beer. I hope you won't mind
Giving me some for I am quite in need of something nice to drink?

Kate would willingly give this lady anything for shelter.
The fog's gone now, but the day is cloud-dark; rain may well pelt her
Later and her sister and the deer must both be kept safe, she thinks.

26.

Liz Raseil gobbles the beer down like it was water then burps.
'You will be happy to stay with me. I have a trough for slurps
Of lusciousness, and a sty for sleeping the sweet sleep of the just!

I cannot wait to bring you there for you will only delight
In what I can offer you. And it will feel as if you might
Want to stay with me forever. Others certainly feel they must!'

Kate senses they are circling now around what must be her home.
She drops the bloodied nightgown round the doe's waist, leaves her alone;
Takes Sophie in her arms, does not notice when the doe goes,

Quietly slips back as they follow this woman of the woods
To her carefully constructed, secret hovel. 'If you could
Go in, I'll latch my door behind you and lock it. Then let the snows

Of winter come! They won't reach us here in my lonely coven
Where I rarely see another soul except those that I have loved and
Turned into sweet little boars to join the rest in the sty beside

My great oak tree. Please don't cry now that I have used my magic.
On you. 'Twill do you no good. I've changed you both too, to tragic
Sowlets to turn on my fire for suckling roasts when deep cold abides.

27.

Be very sure that I have loved you both, you charming dears.
It's why I've rendered you porcine. When I eat you no tears
Will I shed, for you will have both been rescued from a far worse fate.'

They're dazzled by her bright smile as she kicks them into her sty.
Blind to other little pigs pushing for space, deaf to their cries.
Four-leggedly aware she does not hold Sophie anymore, Kate

Sniffs and scents her there just beside her and slowly through the gloom
She recognises what has happened and what will be their doom.
Her anguish sounds as snivellings and snoutings, her cries as snorts.

A dim light filters through the piles upon piles of old branches
Stack-leaned on each other, weighing more than a thousand lances
And Kate tries to think how they might escape, stop their lives being short;

As rain plashing through the leaves outside begins to seep and drip
Down on herself and her comrades in this dark prison. She licks
The back of her sister's head, squeals as another pig bites her bum,

Hopes neither she nor Sophie will be next as the chosen feast
For the witch to eat. It's so crowded here, hard for those least
Able to bite back. Mud-grunting, their animal life's now begun.

28.

Truffle, stool and 'shroom lore helps her next day after a nightmare
Of honking and shuffling fails to make room in this pig-sty lair
For them to lie down and rest. Damp trotters rot in the mud-shit ground.

As the witch fills the trough with silage that afternoon, its stench
Draws their snouts; Kate fight-bites her way through to it, feels like a wench
Scent-searching. She finds apples, plums, acorns for Sophie; is swill-bound

As she chew-grinds and secretes them in her cheeks then drip-feeds her
Runt-sister in this dark, mud-jail. 'Where's the hind when I need her?'
She wonders, noticing her thoughts becoming formless, inchoate

As she defecates in some other pig-child's face without shame
'What is happening to us? I have become brutish, untame,
As if the witch's spell must give both my body and mind disgrace.

What a pity I can not cry. I must just save my sister.'
Sophie's bleats break Kate's heart which bleeds her wish to resist the
Bane-woman whose kindness to orphans she sore-needs to berate.

To hate her would be to join her. In her dim animal brain
Kate still knows this perfectly well, it somehow helps her stay sane.
For a human being. For a young sow she's mad and she's irate.

29.

Liz Raseil's fire is red and black, her cauldron as copper
As the great beech at Tewkesbury. Benevolent and proper,
Her bearing in the woods is, it is clear, of a good woman wronged.

You would never know her elegance is as bought as a frock
From a fashion floor in some department store; nor that she locks
Away memories with the piglets to squeal her betrayal song.

Her daughters disobeyed her, left with their father and friends
For Oxford to be Royalists. Then other men raped her. No end
Then to her shame could there be, but to live in the woods as a witch,

Alone except for her waifs and strays. Alone with her fire.
Alone with her appetite, her insatiable desire
To circle round her need for punishment, to know herself a bitch,

An evil, selfish bane-woman, trapped in time, who loves her own pain;
Love-longs to do what is wrong again and again and again;
Re-shaping compassion, saving children from suffering her fate.

Fair as the fall, she thinks of the green piglet, stares at her flames
Knowing it's better to be dead than emotionally maimed.
Boiled piglet-thoughts make her ruby lips shine and she salivates.

30.

The marrow boy from Hartpury creeps like a cat towards her,
Sees she does not see him, lost in her *abbaisement* disorder,
Clasps his bellarmine jar stuffed with clippings of hair and toenails,

To ward off her wickedness; terrified as he silent-crawls
Behind her stinking, awful sty with its grunts and pig-cries; calls
Quietly to the green sow to retreat from the fired food-pail

Side of her prison. He wants to steal the fire and torch that sty,
Burn a hole for bolting from, knows not 'tis packed, that pigs will die
If he carries out his dim-boy plan. Nor does Kate understand

But she has heard his voice above the mournful porcine hubbub,
Her pig-brain can't compute as she hears him change his mind, start to lug
Branches away from behind the sty with his rough, hard-calloused hands

As quietly as he can. But the bane woman hears his noise,
Snaps from her reverie, x-ray-sees him and smiles. She loves boys,
Picks up her velvet skirts, strides round the sty with her huge torch-candle,

Grinning from ear to beautiful old ear. But before she can turn
His boy-bones to pig's, he grasps her ankle. She slips, her candle burns
Her hair and she pitch-falls, screeching to the ground, all of a tangle.

31.

'Tis she now who holds his ankle, but he hits her on the head
With a branch which is so heavy in his hand it feels like lead.
Her scream might be heard in Africki, so loud is its resonance.

He hits her again. Her sigh is then hushed; he can hear her pain.
Hates what he's doing. Blood from her brow pours down her cheeks like rain.
He hits her again and she mad-smiles to herself as if in a trance.

He stops and stands back. On the ground her red dress, red hair, red blood
Make her pale face and hands and feet merge with the earth and the mud
This dreadful night. Inside the dark, branched sty the piglets howl-squeal.

Hearing the violence without, feeling it like it's within,
Kate waits with bated breath. Her head is beginning to spin
As the sty door is opened and the boy looks in as if they're unreal.

His eyes are wide and his mouth is open, breathing heavily from his fight
And shocked by all the piglets he sees bent-cowering in fright.
'Fear not,' he says, polite. 'I won't cook you. Come out now, run away!'

But they don't. They all stay there, stuck fast, all of them, all shaking
Like leaves on their little legs, afraid, stammering and quaking.
Then a single green one pushes through the throng towards the doorway.

32.

She cannot tell him who she is. She cannot tell herself. Where's
Sophie? Baby Sophie can not yet crawl, but as a pig there's
No stopping her at all waddling after Kate. And the others

Follow her like a burge-stream. The boy sets fire to the hovel
And then to the sty as well. Screaming, the poor piglets grovel,
Gathering round the boy. Blinking, half-blind, they look for their mothers,

Who would not recognise them were they still alive or come here.
Enraged her home is aflame, the now seared-bald witch gets up. Fear
Triggers piglet paranoia – they slip-slide-sprint after the boy.

But Liz Raseil's magic spelling's gone with her confidence.
Her bruised, burned head stings. Her ears ring. She staggers, leans on her fence
Watching her world conflagrate. The fleeing pigs are shrill, their noise

And the smell of smoke has put them into a dreadful panic
They can even taste themselves as pork as they run with manic
Abandon through bracken and brambles towards the broad brown river.

Not that they know that. They stream out after the boy and green pig,
That's all. As they hurtle through the undergrowth some dance a jig,
Their bodies return to those of boys and girls, alert, aquiver.

Engenderings

33.

For dread of the bane woman means they would rather drown than stop.
And the muddy water here is turbulent and strong, will lock
Them into a downward spiral to the bottom if they jump in.

All of them are morphing like cut pumpkins lit at Halloween.
Some still are pigs, some already children now, some in between,
Standing at the river's bank fully prepared to take a dunking

If needs must be, but willing never to let the witch take them
Back. They're so scared of that, that Kate, girl again, though green, makes them
Calm down by singing, but is scared too 'cos she can't see her sister.

Some eighteen children she counts, only one of them hasn't changed yet.
It must be Sophie. Her sigh of relief comes with a long breath let
Out – Sophie's herself again 'midst the other bairns. She's so missed her.

But slope-sliding down into the water with a soundless splash,
Sophie sinks as helpless as a pink stone. Like a grebe, Kate's dash
To dive in after her is faster than her feelings of fear.

The boy jumps in too and then all the other children as well,
As if they could swim and as if they had no choice, truth to tell.
But they can't swim and did have choice. Many will drown it is clear

34.

Swirling in Habren's sinuous twisting currents and churn-rolls,
The children who drown are embraced by eternity's true gold
Certainties; safe from the travails of time, they are free to fly.

Kate is not. Nor yet is the marrow boy whose hand she has got
Searching through these fast-moving muddied waters. She finds her not,
Lets go the marrow-boy in agitation, dives again, must try;

She cannot live without her sister. There'd be no point. She dives
Again and again, is distracted by the frightened, drowning cries
Of other children who can't swim, has to rescue them, saves but two.

Others get turned in the water and bobble up lower down
Face down then disappear forever. Neither a sight nor sound
Of Sophie does she get as bedraggled, wretched, she has to screw

Up her courage and scramble up on to the bank again, look
From there if she can see her, knows in her heart she's forsook.
But clambers up anyway, scans downriver searching for a view.

Soaked, scratched, sore and shivering poor Kate is scorned by the Severn
Whose dispassionate tumbles and twists don't care that her suck-yearn
For her sister is now as deep as her need for her mother too.

138

35.

It wracks her whole body and her sobs sound like cracks in the sky
She nur-wants to hurl herself back into the river and die
As dusk begins to remerge the lengthening shadows into one.

Instead she sits, then starts to slide back in the water. She'll just go.
As the night comes in she'll join her sister in the baleful flow,
Quietly return the embrace that death gives to everyone.

Hands land on her shoulders, halting her. The marrow-boy soft-speaks.
'Please don't,' he says, stopping his dark eyes in his small, tight face, leak
Tears. 'These children are little and trusting. They'll follow you and drown.

Those that don't will die here of cold or the bad lady will take them
Back. Your sister has gone. Accept it, please and help me make them
Safe. Some must live only for others, though it makes us sad and we frown.

When I threw that apple at you I wanted to be different.
Then I had to be true, come after you or be in torment.'
She looks back at him, hates his stench of sanctimony, wants to spit.

Only seven other children are still here. The rest have gone, drowned.
Their sorry little faces reflect her own hurt in the round.
She cannot stay with them. She could not bear it. She does not fit.

36.

Her place is the water, as food for fishes, as slime for stones.
She slides in up to her neck. The marrow boy does too. Not alone,
All the other children do as well. Some cry, but they all can swim,

Their little heads bobbing after hers as she lets herself go.
The water is cold, the current is strong. She's done wrong, she knows.
But here in the watery darkness swept along, her heart can sing

Its song of sorrows. Then she sees a skiff left tied to a tree
And compassion dictates that she cannot only selfish be.
She clambers in. The marrow boy helps each child up and in as well.

Small and shivering in the dark, Kate slips the mooring, lets it drift
Downstream. Shocked and chilled, the children's tired, pale faces start to shift
From despair to small hope, but if they have reason she cannot tell.

She peers out into the trees on both sides, looking for somewhere
They might stop, find shelter, food, warmth, clothing for these bairns
But the night now is dark and she knows they'll all be dead by morning

From cold. The river slaps the skiff, pushes them from swirl to trough
In circles. Through the trees she spies a pale shape and hears a cough
But the river moves them on before her sense of it comes dawning.

37.

'I saw your deer,' says the marrow boy. 'Your sister at its neck
Like a moonstone. How can that be?' Kate's heart hope-starts, eyes scan-check
Every bush and tree. But it's so dark she can hardly see a thing.

The marrow boy grabs hold of a branch overhanging and pulls
Them over to the side. Katie's sister-longing is so full
She can feel nothing except the rhythm of her own heart ringing

Like a bell! Those silver antlers and that white behind belong
To no-one else! Her head is bent down, but it cannot be wrong –
And there's Sophie! Kate and the marrow boy tug tufts till the skiff's 'moored'.

Alighting and slip-running up the grassy mound with more haste
Than sense, not caring her legs get more thorn-scratched, she radiates
Joy for there, beneath the hind's face, her sister lies like a new-born,

Radiant, waving her hands and feet at the hind who licks her
Gently to remove the masses of cling-burrowing ticks her
Little body is covered in. Joy turns to horror. Kate must help.

She picks at ticks all night long. The marrow boy makes a hay bed
For the children covered with dried sedge and leaves and grasses dead.
Above, the sky clears. A new moon is rising, whiting the cloud shelf.

38.

She falls asleep at dawn. The morning star's followed by the sun's
Rise making mist of the dew as they lie there breathing as one
Till the heat of the new day burns it off and, warmed, they can yawn, stretch

And begin to believe that all might be well again one day.
Only one child has died overnight. The strange, pale hind nay-says
When the marrow boy wants to respectfully pick him up and fetch

Him to the river, to wet-bury him. The hind wants Kate to take
Sophie, lay the boy beside her. To the marrow boy, 'I'll make
Space,' Kate says, picking up her sister. 'He's nearly as big as you are,

But lay him by the hind, please, and she will give him succour, bring
Him back to life by finding who he is and giving him wings
With which to help him fly back here from beyond the river of stars!

So let's take off his damp clothes to dry in the sun. Mam's nightgown
Will do for him for now; he can put them back on when the hind's found
His life back for him again.' With Sophie safe-tucked back in her arms

Everything feels wonderful on this lovely golden morning.
Late autumn apples and berries, yellow and purple, warm in
The sun. If Kate could be an oak sapling, it's doing her no harm.

39.

A small girl wants to hold Sophie, drip blackberry juice on her lips.
Kate gives her with a smile, but thinks we'll never survive this trip
Without the hind. The baby's tick scars are everywhere and livid.

Grateful, but curious, she asks the marrow boy for his name.
He tells her he doesn't have a personal one, is ashamed
He's only called 'boy'. He does have a family name. 'It's vivid

Enough and says what my family do. We're undertakers.
My family name's Bier.' 'Well, I'll be your own name-maker
Then! Can I call you, if you'd really let me… can I call you… Paul?'

His nod is shy. And she knows why. They are about the same age.
'How old are you, Paul?' 'I do not know. My father was not sage
Enough to tell me.' 'Well, I feel that, though compared to you I'm small,

We are much the same age. I have fourteen summers. So must you,
I think. What will you do now? Will you return home? I trust you
Will not meet Mrs Raseil on the way; if you do, be careful.'

The marrow boys thanks her, but says that now he has a name he'll
Be pleased to stay with Sophie and herself, protect them, or kill
Those who'd do them harm. But of violence Kate has had her share-full.

40.

The children are still, listening as the morning sun shines down.
They none of them know where they come from, what village nor what town.
The boy who was dead is standing now in her mother's bloody nightgown.

He goes over to the wild hedgerow where Paul had hung his clothes
And delves in his brown jerkin pocket for something that he knows
He must recover. He finds it. It gleams in the sun, small and round.

'What's that, Lazarus Boy?' Paul asks. 'You who've been brought back from death.'
'It's my dad's signet ring,' the Laz-boy replies. 'My living breath
Is due to the beautiful white hind. I want her to have my ring.

He slips it over an antler. It sparkles in the sunlight
Beside the twiggy doll. The other children take great delight
The doe's become bedecked. Around her they begin to dance and sing.

This Laz-boy must be gentry, with his sense of duty, Kate's sure,
Musing on his 'death' she wonder-asks where they are. 'Maisemore,'
Paul replies. 'A mile west, maybe. Wherever you go I shall too.'

'Thank you for your kindness but we're bound for family in Wells
The hind will take us.' Paul points at the children. 'What shall we tell
Them? Must they now face being homeless, orphaned – know that awful truth?'

41.

'They cannot come with us and nor can you! They must go back home.
And you must too!' She rounds on the children who look more alone
As the feel-meaning of her words reminds them of how lost they are.

They've stopped dancing round the hind, look at her without reproach, sad
Though perplexed. Kate ignores them, attends to Sophie, feeling mad
Herself at what she's caused. But what to do now her purpose is marred?

She cannot go without them but they cannot come too. She's vexed
Now, would love to be able to put a spell on them, a hex
Which could take them back to a gentler time when they were cared for, loved.

But she is no witch. Though, like some witch, she is ever so green.
It cannot be for no reason that her skin now is as it seems.
Power to change these children into a flock of grey turtle doves

Who could fly where they would, would be wonderful. Paul says 'Alright,
I'll go west with them. We learned we can ride in that skiff last night.
I'll take them to Bristol, leave them by a church or down at the docks.

You'd best come with us for a while. Habren'll take us all the way.
You should leave at Minsterworth, I think. Keep the sun of midday
To your right. But, no! You'll have the hind to take you! You'll need no clock'

42.

The hind and Laz-boy with Sophie in his arms, are in the boat
Already. Kate, Paul and the little ones pile in after. Coats,
Blankets and shelter they have none. They are lucky the sun is high,

That this October had been a kind one so far without frost.
Kate thinks of ghosted Mam dying to save the deer. 'We're not lost
While we stay on this skiff together. After that the end is nigh!

Paul says and she looks at him askance. He's a jester and fool
This pall-bearer, Paul Bier. She would rather ride on a mule
To Wells than go with him much further! He unties the mooring rope.

They begin to drift. The land here is much flatter, less treed, more reeds
They could see and could be seen if there are bad men here who lead
Lives of revenge and rapine and hatred of bairns (for they mean hope

In the future). The water, as ever, fast-flows, plunges, turns,
Muddy and brown, but twisting and pulling it moves so fast, churns
Around itself like it's always being poured, never settles or pools.

The children and the white hind find themselves being swept around
And around, often the skiff brushes the bank and scrapes the ground
But such is the rush of the river they never stop. It is cruel.

43.

'What's that round your neck?' Kate, dizzy from rudderlessness, asks Paul.
'It's my bellarmine jar for warding off witches. It is all
I need to make evil depart. It stopped Mrs Raseil's harming!'

'What's inside it?' 'Hair, toenails, stuff! It won't do you any harm.'
'How do you know? I am green,' she says, excited, far from calm.
'Don't you see? Like a plant! Even Liz Raseil found me alarming.'

Habren's current carries them so fast Kate's words get left behind
As she ponders on what has happened to herself and the hind:
Her viridity's permanent; as the hind can't be hart again.

But Paul nor the Laz-boy nor the other children seem bothered
By a girl with green skin and an antlered white doe. Her mother'd
Have been if she could see her now. But then and now are not the same.

'That's St George's church, Minsterworth, ahead,' says tall Paul Bier
As one who knows. For some reason, Kate feels a chill and can hear
The hind's anxiety, stress-pawing at the boards. 'Don't run amock,

Dear,' Kate says. 'There'll be nobody trying to hunt you from a church.'
And as they drift downstream the skiff is drawn towards it. Alert
For danger, they are thrown forward when it thump-bumps on the church rock.

44.

The skiff lodges up against it, firmly jammed by the current.
'I'll get us free,' Paul says. 'But first I will find some cerements
Here – winding sheets to wrap up in to keep us all cosy and warm!'

Kate knows not what he's talking about, neither do the others,
But twixt church and three yews, sloops are busy loading fruit. Cover
Would be nice now the sun is going down. Still, adults can do harm

So 'twould be best to move on. But Paul runs past apple-growers
Boat builders, sailors of sloops and matelots. All seem slower
About what they do than he is and Kate sure-hopes he won't be too long.

And, yes, he is back in no time with shrouds and water and bread!
'My cousin lived here. His mam let me have all this 'cos he's dead;
Died of plague. She said keep them, but I told her it would be wrong

As I'm giving up pall bearing and will undertake no more
In my life again. I'll bring the sheets back one day, I am sure.
This pail is for eels. There are hundreds in the church for us to cook.'

Telling the Laz-boy to look after the rest, Kate follows him
Along the landing. High tide flooded the church this morning. They skim
Eels from the floor of its nave. So many they hardly have to look.

45.

Kate is amazed. 'My aunt said they come from the Sargasso Sea,'
Paul says. 'The sailors told her. Maybe they've come for you and me
And the bairns, specially! It's May they should arrive. Not now!' Kate feels faint.

Rather than collapse she sits down on a pew, her head is spinning,
She wants to be sick. Paul asks her if all this eel-binning
Is getting to her, but she's passed out, swooned. His deep concern's unfeigned

As he lifts her on his shoulder, the pail in his other hand
And carries her back down the inlet path to the skiff. 'You can
Help me lift her in,' he says to the laz-boy, gives him the large pail

Of eels first and then together they soft-place her in the bow.
The hind too is suffering, her cries make a terrible row.
Paul jumps in and he casts off worried that the matelots will rail

'Gainst him, tell him he's mad taking children in an overloaded skiff
Downstream. They don't. And Kate and the hind quick-get better, as if
Nothing happened. Kate, puzzled, remembers not what occurred in church

And when Paul tells her, frowns. 'I think,' she says. 'That now I am green,
In church I'm not allowed. And just looking at your Bellarmine
Jar makes the hind and me pall. Please throw it away, Paul, lest we lurch!'

46.

And he does; pulls it off and hurls it in the river. They drift,
Sharing bread beneath the winding sheets, Paul's aunt's generous gift.
They start to sing again. The skiff slowly spins. The river broadens.

The current burgeons. Marsh Tits and Peewits watch Willow Warblers
Gather, late to leave, above the trees. These and other dawdlers
Who've lingered too long will see the sun set as the wide sky yawns

On the rumbling, directed turbulence of the Bore sweeping
Upstream towards the current-carried skiff, unaware, leaking
At its gunwhales, with the weight of these orphaned children, of its doom.

But the eels know. They are seething in their bucket, they feel
The ignominy of it, going downstream again. Their real
Task was to die up here. They are revived, singing a conjoint tune

Of distress about being pailed to face the Bore rather than run with it.
Having already swam thousands of miles they'd reached the limit,
As they thought, of what they had to do and this is desecration

Therefore. Their bucket starts to bubble behind the hungry bairns
Who do not notice them pouring out; so desperate, they yearn
To return to the river and swim back to their destination.

47.

Their duty is to die. The children must also follow fate's
Decrees as they try as well to assert their own will to make
Time and space bend to their particular needs, hopes and desires.

Most are feeling, as they chew their bread, the parents that they've lost,
There's nought they can do but ride the river wherever they're tossed.
Except for Kate who's that much older and sure she can use her ire

To do what she wants. 'You three can stop off at Newnham,' says Paul.
'Then find somewhere to sleep and tomorrow be on your way. Shawls
And blankets you might not have, but I will give you a winding sheet.'

'Thank you, Paul. Since you threw that jar I've been feeling much stronger.
We met no bad men in Minsterworth. Peace has lasted longer
Perhaps, away from Corse Lawn? To feel safe and sound is such a treat!'

The skiff scuffs some stones and mud. Paul pushes away from the bank
And sits Sophie on his knee to watch late birds in vast serried ranks
Fly to the sunset before turning south... Time's pattern does not slip.

The slap and slurp of water on wood and the gathering dusk
Together make them feel quite safe. Some of them sleep, have no lust
To stay awake, would be pleased to dream till dawn, drift down to Cardiff.

48.

They don't know the whole channel twixt Wales, Devon and Somerset
Funnels currents and streams, that south to north, have crossed the whole planet;
That the largest seas and the hugest waves have climbed over the oceans

To send their strength finally in one great Bore whose ripple roar
Resounds like the penis of the lord of all creations; sure
In its penetration as the sun is of the sky's motion

Around it in Cerulean adulation of its blinding
Power. They do not know Noadu rides a seahorse, finding
The crest of the wave of all waves which will drown the whole world one day.

Then leave. They do not know time is concertinaed, that Quartets
From Elliot, Arks from Noah, Quantum rhymes, trains from Morpeth,
And *All* else will be engulfed by the rising of this wondrous wave

Which surge-washes Qiantang, Pororoca, indifferent
To the conceits of place or name, or people; as if it's sent
To defy gravity, drown the world and then drop off into space.

They do not know that 'one day' is today, nor why it should be
Overwhelming death's disparate dealings emotionally
Is what we are really here for, is why we joined the human race.

49.

Habren's a woman and knows what it is like to have the bore
Caress her banks as he mounts her with controlled power which is more
To do with her holding him to task than it is with his release.

Her meadows with alder and sedge and mud-marsh ossier beds
Make it so easy to hold him, take his thrusts between her legs
And let him come inside her and, if he must, make flood. She feasts

On his smooth, rhythmed persistence rip-rumbling along the length
Of her sex. She loves his touch sounding along her floor. Her strength
Is her ability to take in everything he's got to give

And more, as he makes his way up inside her. Sloops and skiffs may
Float on her surface, motor boats too in years to come, but say
The bore doth run and she ripple-quivers, knows what it is to live.

The bore has come. Ravishing her depths and surfacing,
He lifts her in a surge-tide of sensation, strokes her basin
As she bears down passionately on his lustrous intention to shoot

And makes of it a dissipating slurry as he hurries
To his anti-climactic end just shy of Tewkesbury,
With the merest shudder, lick-lapping her rocks and stones, mud and roots.

50.

What of Kate, Sophie, the Laz-boy, Paul, the little ones, the hind?
Between Broadoak and Newnham they are pushed by the bore and find
They're surf-giddy, sent in a great slow-rush right back to Maisemore

In circles which make all except Kate, the Laz-boy and the hind feel sick.
As if being green, returning from death, and changing sex, tricks
The Bore and somehow makes these three immune to nature's normal laws.

But Paul and the little ones moan and cry, groan, vomit, and scream,
Terrified and dizzy all at the same time. Like in a dream
They feel. So when the bore's finally done, they all fall fast asleep.

Wrapped in their winding sheets, they look so vulnerable that Kate,
The hind and the Laz-boy cannot bear to wake them. It's so late
Now, all is dark except for the light cast by the hind. The skiff streaks

Along though; carried downstream once more by Habren's current's urgent
Need now to flow back to sea. Past Elmore, Newnham, Fretherne, sent
As speedily as starlight, they are, even though they have no oars.

Habren broadens as her waters flow towards the ocean. She
Becomes so wide and her flow so strong that the small skiff's made tiny.
Wide-awake, Kate is fearful, far from safe, out here in Habren's maw.

51.

Three of the children, two boys, are nearly as green as she is.
The sorry skiff's a damp rag of a thing; burial cloth-ends drift-
Dangle over the side; they're so cold and ill, they can barely groan.

Slopping with sick, salt water and one or two eels, the skiff
Has sped through the night past Bristol, Redwick, out to sea, Cardiff
Is North North West before dank grey morning beaches them at Flat Holm.

Not that they know that. Any of them. In fact it takes a while
Before they even notice they're not floating anymore. Miles
From home they don't realise they've stopped bobbing and moving, are stuck

Still In silt. It's Paul who first observes that their boat is stuck fast,
That the hind is standing in blue tufts of wind-blown wire grass
On solid ground, brown eyes wide, as if astounded at their luck,

Or lack thereof; looking almost sheepish! Paul wakens Katie.
Her green skin all goose-bumped, she looks like a fish who's just lately
Been caught. 'I think we had better wake everyone up and dry the sheets

In the wind. Maybe the sun will come out!' Paul says, 'Warm us up!'
'You are a fool, Paul, with your attempts at good cheer. But we must tuck
Into the last of our bread and get warm, then Wells we must seek.

52.

Will you come too? There is no point now in separating.
You can't look after these bairns on your own, make reparation
For their motherlessness, without help from one just as abandoned.

Yes, I do mean me! Come on! Let's be on our way. I'll be glad
Not to have to sit in this boat a moment more!' Scarcely clad,
And huddled beneath the long winding sheets, the little ones were conned

Into sleep last night by the rhythm of the water rocking
Them downstream. Now, in this bleak, cold sea-dawn there is no stopping
The exposure killing them. Their cries are rare, muted, weak, forlorn.

As Paul and Kate help them out of the skiff, carry them across
And lay them down on not-quite dry land by the hind. 'We're not lost,'
Kate tries to placate their dismalings. 'You will later feel reborn

When we have found you new homes with wonderful new mams and dads
To love you and feed you and keep you warm! You lasses and lads
Will be so glad you came here with us, that then we found you a home!'

She's glad her words go with the wind – she hears how hollow they sound.
The children are limp and cold, it's not long till dead they'll be found.
Paul reads a sign, drawls, 'We're on an island – Flat Holm,' his voice like stone.

53.

Marooned. The Cymbran coast's north of them, Somerset's to the south
But all they see is sea all around, burge-foaming like the mouth
Of the solitary black Ox, nostrils flared, tethered to a post

Behind them. The sea's flecked, running like the eels of yesterday
In channelled, sinewed rivulets, thousands of shades of grey,
Which roll round and over each other, merging into one, almost.

'We're going to die here, aren't we?' The Laz-boy says, half-bewildered
But not stupid. He can see what's going on and like a builder
Mimes the shape of what's to come if they can't get off, mock-'slits' his throat.

Paul says, 'Perhaps you can live forever since you've conquered death.'
The Laz-boy's shivering uncontrollably, is out of breath.
He shakes his head, looks at the little ones. 'We're wet, we have no coats.

We'll die.' He helps Kate and Paul lay out each winding sheet full length
On the ground to dry, placing shingle in heaps at either end
In case the great sea winds should come and sweep them up, blow them away.

But for now on this cold grey morn all is still. The tide goes out.
The children are ill, most of them, and no help is about.
The incremental ice-chill of imminent unfair death pervades.

54.

But still all is still, save for the breath of the Ox making mist
From his nostrils all around Flat Holm. Its tendrils gently twist
And insinuate themselves everywhere. Like sea currents they curl

And merge in a blanket above which only Kate and Paul's heads
Are tall enough to see the Ox's eyes are reproachful and red,
But then he dips his head into the mist and is gone in a whirl.

Kate knows that look, though she has not seen it for more than eight years.
It's the look her father had whenever noises made him fear
For their lives before he was stabbed by poachers, dyed the green grass red.

It's the colour of Dad's last look at them, lying there dying;
He'd been so worried, as his blood poured out, they'd be left crying
And alone with no-one to feed and protect them after he was dead.

She'd been more upset by how distressed he was, than that he'd gone
When eventually he did depart, sent by Mam's tears which shone
With all the years she would live without him before she too would die.

But now the Ox is shrouded in mist she looks across at Paul
Knowing 'tis reproach of the living that makes him snort and call.
His heavy hoof-steps across the sand and shingle just make her sigh.

55.

But Paul's terrified. 'That Ox will kill us and he's coming this way.
How did he get free? And how can we save the bairns this awful day?'
Kate gives him her Viridiana smile, says, 'They'll be safe with you.

The Ox has been left here to die. He's not going to stomp or gore
Anyone. He wants to hang his chain on the hind's antlers or
Maybe just be with us for his last look into the void of blue.

Before leaving this world for his Merging. I heart-know his breath
Is magical, somehow, via Sophie. He'll bring life not death
To the little ones as he expires! I know! I really do!'

As she speaks the Ox's looming presence rears out of the mist.
She greets him with a friendly smile, clearly feels that there's no risk,
Paul observes, as if in a dream of something other, something true.

As the morning sun burns the mist off Flat Holm and turns everything
Autumn Azure, the Hind's in the sand warming the bairns. This brings
A surge of hope to Katie and Paul as the big black Ox stands still,

Taking in the light and the life all around him. The green girl
Steps forward, unscrews the silver chain from his nose, turns, and curls
It round the Hind's antlers like limetta. 'All will be well, it will!'

56.

She speaks happily, beaming with delight at her arrangement.
Behind her the Ox lands with a great thump on his side. Estrangement
From this world went with his chain. He lies on his side like a beached whale.

'All will be well,' Kate repeats. 'The Hind knows. She's telling me so.
Secretly. Don't be scared! We'll line our skiff with the Ox hide, go
Back to sea when the tide's coming in, and then to land we'll sail!'

Behind her cheerful facade she's frightened, truly wants no more
To see innards steam after the horrors of Corse Lawn, abhors
The prospect more than she longs to see her kind auntie Jane again.

Anyway they have no knife. Her joy's the bairns have been restored
Since the Ox's passing. They have risen with the sun. Adored
By Kate for their resilience, she makes them hold hands, then exclaims,

'The Ox seems to have given you his energy now he's died.
Let us walk round the island and while we're on the other side
Paul and the Laz-boy can... find razor shells! And flay the Ox's hide!'

'Just like that!' the Laz-boy says. Kate asks him his name, eyebrows raise'd.
'I'm a bastard son of Lionel Cranfield. My name's Gervase.
I've been brought back from death, but that doesn't mean I can't be snide.'

57.

Acknowledging this with a curt smile, Kate makes her green hue red
For a brief, involuntary moment, wants to hate; instead
She re-gathers her vegetative state and recalls he's her friend,

She says, 'Paul can do it by himself then, I suppose, if you want.
Would you like instead to walk with us?' Babes at the baptismal font
Would seem less innocent than these bairns' gladness they don't face their end!

They reach for his hand eagerly. He smiles, calm again, demurs.
She shrugs, leads the bairns along the sand and shingle, feels cursed
Being green, but happy too to have understood both bull and hind,

And to be alive with these children this wondrous sunny day.
The sun is almost as warm as summer on her face. 'Let's play
Here,' she says. The little ones hurray-say she's a lady so kind

As she rocks Sophie in her arms. 'Not yet a woman, just a girl,'
She replies, but they laugh and say she's a leaf lady and twirl
And dance across the dunes, so full of life, her heart's aflame with joy.

She glances out to sea again. The tide's doubly receded
It's waterless now between Flat Holm and Cymbran. We've needed
Just such conditions, she thinks, relieved. I must go back to the boys,

58.

Stop them skinning the Ox, show them the absent sea, quickly talk
About fearing taking the leaky old skiff, suggest we can walk
– walk! – to Cymbran right now! If we really hurry, it can be done!

She claps her hands, which perturbs poor Sophie, calls out, 'Little ones!
Come back to me! We must return fast to the big boys then run
As quick as we can – cross the wet sands faster than light from the sun!

But they play on, toy with jetsam and heap up a pile of stones,
Laughing and happy to be alive. Kate smiles too, does not moan,
For the sea still goes out – impossibly far – this beautiful day.

If you could look down from on high you would surely be worried.
Deep down, miles below, mountains below, the mid-Atlantic seas,
In the middle of the ocean, Earth's floor is rupturing in twain,

Splitting from itself as forces deeper than the sea quake-shake the world
All unknown in the morning sun to these children and this girl
Who build a cairn for the kindness of the Ox who lay down his life.

You'd urge the two big boys to work faster removing its hide,
Ignore their revulsion sawing through his jaw and breast, confide
That they must hurry, launch the skiff before the tidal wave strikes.

59.

But the high you are looking down from exists in time not space.
Though these children know much about trials for the human race
They have never heard of great Tidal Waves or Continental Shelves.

The little ones are piling stone upon stone, have made a mound
On Flat Holm, this sun-lovely day, which then they all sit around
While Kate, across the way, speaks with Paul and Gervase, 'We must not dwell

In this time like there's always tomorrow. If we cross the bed
Of sand and mud, rocks and wrecks we'd be back on dry land ahead
Of the tide coming back in. Then all will be well and we'll be safe!'

With their hands and fronts all covered in blood the two big lads stand
And look at where she's pointing. 'The sea has gone! There's just wet sand
Betwixt us and dry land,' she says, all excited. 'Let's take the waifs

And cross it while we can!' Paul agrees, but the Lazarus boy
Whose name's Gervase, says nay, while he was dead it was his strange joy
To see all times and all space: knows if they cross now they'll be drowned.

'Unless, we're not! For I saw all and everything of all that could be.
Strange to say: all that is, could not be; yet all at once would be
At the same time everywhere! So skinning the Ox would be more sound.

60.

At least... All we can trust is what we feel, and that's what I feel.'
The hind gets to her feet from the sand and stands behind his heels.
Her white fur's troubled. Her bedecked antlers gleam. She supports his words.

Kate knows in her bones that he's right, but she's desperate to try
And get away now. In her head she feels they're certain to die
If they do not leave now. She looks at the sky blackening with birds.

Crazy as frogs with wings, they're heading every which way in flocks.
It's mad. Many of them are crashing into each other and drop
Like stones into the mud-sand. Kate screams, 'We'll stay here no longer!'

She screams so loud that all the little ones sitting round their cairn
Jump up and run to her. 'We're off. We're leaving now, little bairns,
You must come with us, Paul. With you with us we'll cope and be stronger

When little ones struggle.' 'No!' Gervase says. 'We must skin the Ox.
Please Paul, stay.' But Paul's heart belongs to Kate and he won't be rocked.
'I can't let the little one's cross that soggy, gullied sand without guilt.

Not on their own.' Kate's relieved to hear this, sweeps up the smallest
To join Sophie in her arms, says, 'Come on, then, let's go, Tallest
First! So he – you Paul! – can reach for my hand if down a hole, you're spilt!'

61.

Her laugh scorns him and they set off gingerly north to Cymbran
Gervase watches, then attends to his saw-cutting. He's pale, wan,
As skuas, sheerwaters, gannets and gulls continue to collide

And crash down around him as he goes on with his grizzly work.
It's as if the dead Ox helps him. It gets so easy he smirks
As he finally pulls back the last part, rip-strips carcass from hide

Then carries it to the skiff, looking as raw-flayed as he feels.
Should it be outside in or inside out – food for fish and eels?
He really does not know. He'd ask the hind, but she just sighs,

And looks anxiously after Kate, Paul and the children walking.
Gervase looks too, counts. One's missing. The rest are urgent-talking.
But they are that far away now he cannot hear their frightened cries.

He lays the skin inside out in the boat, presses it in place.
Behind him the carcass, like flies on a meal with no plate,
Is being peck-devoured by a passing flock of ravens or crows.

He does not care and does not know. Far away over there
On the grey splotched ripples of mud and white sand he sees four bears.
No!!! Oxen – A team being driven by someone whose head's aglow!

62.

In the middle of the bottom of the strange now sea-less sea
Katie is holding back her sobs. Paul, her marrow boy, is deceased.
He was blithe-stepping ahead, cheering them to follow, when he sank

Slowly down a grey glutinous suck-hole of soft wet quicksand
Which belched, having taken him, just as he'd said with upraised hands,
'Come no further, Kate. Hold back the little ones. We had no romance

But I loved to serve you, would have done anything, even died
For you, and now I find I am dying! I'll be washed by tides
Turning over me. It was as if you knew I would be swallowed!

And sure enough it's coming to pass, my legs are being pulled
Ever downwards and there is no bottom. My beating heart's full
Of anxiety now, face to face with this way all must follow.

But I'm so frightened to die, Katie, having hardly lived.
I feel like I have failed – dying so young. Fallen through the sieve
Before my time could come. I hope you get to your auntie in Wells.

I'm so afraid. I should be sad the Hind's not here to save me
I don't know why I'm not. I can face it, yet don't go bravely
Into any good night! And I hate having no choice, truth to tell.

63.

I am becoming something else, something lost and gone. Go back
To Gervase on Flat Holm. Get in the boat and wait. You'll not lack
Water soon. I flush-feel it coming, my bones and blood are rumbling.

Hurry! A great wave surely comes! You must be ready to float
When it arrives, not drown in its rushing to lift up the boat.
It'll take you back on the crest of its surge, surfing not tumbling.

Run, Green Girl, with your baby sister and these children. God's speed
I would wish you if you were half-Christian, but I'll just say heed
The hind's instincts, her senses will carry you to your aunt's resort.'

The deep sea mud swathes Paul's neck. He utters his last earthly words,
'Bye Kate. All's well, as you said, and will always be. That's absurd
Cos I'm being drawn down to death, but it's as true as my life's short!'

'All will be well.' How bitter she feels hearing her words come back
To her as if she could ever have known what would be. She's wracked
By anger with herself, decides that she will go on hunger strike

As a protest against a fate that condemns the innocent
With the same random lack of interest as the guilty when
As humans we have moral choice. She ur-knows what she doesn't like.

64.

The children stand stock still with Kate, their hands in their mouths, eyes wide,
Watching Paul's eyes mirror their own, death-staring up at the sky
As the vacuum in his watery sand-hole sucks him slowly down.

Then it's like he was never there. A small meniscus is all.
A slight breeze coming from the west ruffles its surface. Kate calls
His name aloud, wants to stare at the sun, hating her hollow sound.

Instead she gathers the bairns around her, says they must do as Paul said,
Turns them round as the blue sky deepens, hustles them along, dread
Driving her to push them, fast as she can, ignore piscine corpses

And fields of stranded starfish in this sinewed, soggy Sahara.
The outline of a rotting hulk reminds her of her father
Lying dead – he was, Mam had said, a victim of evil forces.

Then she realises the crabs, mudskippers and stranded seaweed
Are familiar, but not this sunken ship. No! I don't need
To be lost. Not now and here, but I am. She cries, 'we too will die.'

Giving Sophie to Brilliana, the oldest girl, (maybe
All of nine years old), she says, 'please, try to be a big lady
Hold my sister while I climb this upturned boat, see where Flat Holm lies.'

65.

The western horizon is silvered beneath the still high sun,
Shimmers in a fizzing line far away. But not here for fun,
Kate scans all the pools and snaking channels abandoned by the sea

Which are all grey on evanescent grey and try as she may
She can see no flat land with a boy and a skiff. What to say
To the bairns when she slides down again? 'Whatever will be will be'?

But hadn't she known how poor Paul would die before it happened?
Hadn't her insistence he come too, lead the way, set a pattern
Which had trammelled him towards his death? So should she leave these bairns
now?

Wouldn't they be safer without her? She's led them here, it's true,
Perhaps now she's green it's her duty to kill them? Her thinking skewed,
Her heart's heavier than her father's tombstone as she slides back down.

With the image of Paul's submerged face in her mind she knows she's evil.
What can she do? Her shame is she is what she is. Poor Paul's still
Dead and it's still her fault. She can't bear herself now, must reparate

Somehow; but first she must leave these poor little waifs to their fate.
Without her they might have a chance, but she will contaminate
That if she stays. With a tear for Sophie she knows she must separate.

66.

As Kate leaves them Brilliana calls out, 'Kate, why must you go?'
'I am going to find the sea, Brilly. It should be here, as we know.
When I find it I'll tell it to wait, not come back till you're all safe.'

Knowing it is nonsense, even cruel to deceive the young,
She says, 'Just call me if you need me. With my ears and your lungs
I'm sure to hear you and I will come back. So leave now, little waifs

And make your way back to Gervase at Flat Holm. You know the way.
No, don't look at me like that. You do! You know that if you stay
Walking with the sun on your right shoulder – this one – he will hear you

If you shout! Just keep shouting as you walk and stay clear of pools
Of water-sand. You'll be there in no time! It will be like school's
Out, lessons over, and you're going home! Seeing him will surely cheer you!

Go now!!! Go!! I must walk towards the sun to get to the sea,
I think. But hurry up! Off you go! We'll meet again shortly!'
It's good to lie, see their little faces hope-light up at this dare.

'Go on! Yes. Bye-bye!' They all look at her with trepidation.
'Go on,' she shouts and trudge-turns west, past ambergris formations,
Air-drowned basking sharks, bloated bladder fish, clams and crabs everywhere.

67.

The ebbs and flows of time, narrow and broaden, rise and fall
Into particled waves as she walks, head high, dignified, tall
In her will to acc-embrace her shame, like suicide from a cliff.

She walks head hung down in a dispirited state of grieving
For her mother, for Paul and for the children she is leaving
Here beneath the sealess sea; doesn't see she's in a geoglyph,

Of ancient drowned streets washed by the full surge-force of the gulf stream
Over decades of decades down the years. Her heart only keens
For the ones she has lost. She could-would scream, but it would not serve.

Not now, as times collide in an all-encompassing huge stillness,
And hang suspended, like cancers in remission, over this mess
She has made. Far off she hears the children's shoutings for Gervase curve

Like rainbows of sound across the stillness of this golden day
Motivating her to face the sea which has gone, run away
West, as if there's some great chasm out there which has swallowed it whole

She will go there, trudge through sand, slime and mud towards the sunset.
As she does, time slides back thirty five years before her mam was yet
Born. Each sluggish footstep towards the sun's heavier than her soul.

68.

Julio Cortasor describes flitting through time as a 'Bunuel'
Well, these abject, shout-singing orphans in the Bristol Channel
Now have the seventeenth century's eighth year 'Bunueling' them.

And out of time, from Timelessness itself comes the Mighty King
Of Cymbran, Hu, driving his black oxen quartet, crown sparkling
In the late afternoon sun. Looking for afanc, he finds some children

Instead; wonders how, out here in this huge basined, emptied sea
This can be. The first one's a lone wrack-girl for whom he feels pity
Seeing her below walking towards the sea. She must want to die.

A short way away five little ones are calling and walking
Towards a sixth working on a skiff and carefully talking
Back to them from his boat, his voice and his words acting as their guide.

He has lined the boat with the black skin of Hu's former lead ox
Who's clearly now died. The beaded eyes of carrion crows mock
His team with the certainty that in time their time will also come.

Above, shearwaters, terns, kittywakes all wheel with all the birds
Already panic-flying crazily and crashing like words
Which will never be heard again, now the sea's life seems to be done.

69.

Is it done? Hu has never seen anything like this before
In all his aeons. This vast, sodden moonscape breaks all the laws
Of nature. He should have stayed searching in the high mountains and tarns

For the fearsome afanc, but was drawn here where the sea should be
And now finds defenceless orphans the afanc would surely eat
If 'tis down here. He will have to save them, take them back to Cymbran

Let the childless of his many queens squabble over them, peck
Each other for the chance of care-adopting them. He'll collect
The tang-green girl first, she's clearly mad with grief, listless-trudging west.

He whips his red-eyed oxen over hillocks on the sea floor
Trying to get round in front of her to stop her, like a closed door,
From going any further towards the sea away from the rest.

As he whips he watches with his peerless gaze a wonder-wall
Of mountain-high sea loom in the distance. The girl looks so small
Walking unseeing through the angled remnants of this sunken town

He dim-recalls was a thriving port millennia ago.
Standing high on his chariot before her he looks down, knows
She won't understand his words. He shakes his head, folds his arms and frowns.

70.

But she stares right through him as if he is an apparition,
Carries on approaching, as if he's not there, a mere vision.
Behind him, Hu hears a sound bigger than all thunder rumbling

Begin to well up from every corner of the west. His beasts
Snort their anxiety about it, their red eyes wild. The least
He can do is scoop up the green girl, then make them all safe. Fumbling

With his whip, he reaches down, lifts poor Katie up to join him.
She must feel she's dreaming, is his thought, speed-driving his team in
Towards Flat Holm now where the other bairns are sitting in their boat.

'Hurry,' he says to her, helping her down from his chariot
'There's a wave that goes round the world and little time have you got,
Before it reaches here. It's too late to get back to land. Just hope

That your little boat will ride it when it comes. All I can do
With my kingly power is make a feather of you, lift you
All into the air on my afanc-scaring, magical breath, deal

With the power of the wave and with wafting you in the air
As if I had god-like powers not this cod-like despair
Which actually leaves me chasing afancs feeling lonely and unreal.'

71.

Hu's never too sure that his god-like powers aren't a figment
Of his own imagination. But no fantasy pigment
Colours this girl so sickly nor makes the others' faces so pale.

So it's not him they should be scared of, he thinks resentfully.
It's the great wave that's but a mile away now, his far-sight sees.
Its continuous crash and boom's like the sound of all the world's whales

Beaching on the shale all at once. But the green girl hasn't moved.
She's standing where he's put her down, clearly doesn't have a clue
What's going on. 'One of you, leave your boat, come here and get your friend.'

Their fear of him keeps them still. The white deer silently steps up,
Gently nudges the girl towards the boat. With a bit of luck
She might be in before the wave arrives. This can not be their end.

Brilliana reaches out, takes Kate's hand and tries to pull her
On board as the hind pushes. Gervase, whose strength is much fuller
Than Brilly's, helps to hoist her in. Kate herself is dissociate.

She doesn't look at King Hu, as all the rest do, as he blows
A huge welsh mountain wind under their skiff, lifts it from below
On a cradle of breath. The great wave looms. Time to embrace their fate.

72.

The wondrous wall of water is three trees high or maybe more,
Thinks Gervase. It's blotting out the sun. Even the highest tor
Would be drowned if it were not washed away. He loud-shouts out, 'Be Brave!'

But he would not have been heard had he been as loud as thunder
For the Bristol Channel's refilling. Norms are torn asunder:
There's an on-going sonic boom. They're airborne now and might be saved.

But the water-wall's rising up higher in its forward-race.
The loaded skiff's like a little swift as it rises apace.
King Hu keeps blowing upwards down below. Deathlessness his burden –

His lingering hope's killing afanc and saving innocents
Will someday release him from his eternal life punishment.
In the meantime there's nought his immortality isn't worse than.

His breath becomes greater than all the earth's winds joined together.
He blows; sees them make the wave crest high above with great pleasure,
Knowing his own fate will always be to search and never to find.

To find would be to die and that he can never do, even here,
Now, under the in-rushing sea. He sets his cart without fear
For Trawsfynnyd, laughing to have done for nothing something kind.

Engenderings

73.

In the skiff the orphans, except for Katie who's mind has gone,
Are perched between fear and exhilaration, singing a song
With Gervase as he holds on, clinging, to the helm for dear life.

Surfing helplessly on a twenty metre high Tidal Wave
Leaves you in the laps of all the gods. 'Can we,' you have to pray,
'Ever survive this?' as it crush-churns everything, sweeps all aside,

Surging you across continental shelves. Indonesia
Twenty oh four, or Atlantis of collective amnesia,
Or the gigantic slippage of Cumbre Veija on La Palma…

All of these and more take us and our loved one's away. And why?
So the power of powerlessness looks the gods in the eye
Certain that love and care mean more than brute power. So we're calmer

Feeling this in our hearts, even as the wave washes over us all
World-wide, through History, when-wherever random nature would fall
On us, sweep us up as atoms, remind us we're drops in oceans.

We know in our hearts that what matters is how we love and care
For each other; and even in death this soul truth sets us fair
To face mortal exigencies in our world of time and motion.

74.

Rising even higher, closing on the shore, the Tidal Wave
Races over sand banks, rocks, buildings and quays, shingle and shale.
As wide as the eye can see its massive momentum destroys all

In its path; which is the breadth and spread of the whole region
As far inland as forever would be if drowning was legion
And here, now, in sixteen oh seven few will survive this death call.

The tiny ones in the small skiff are screaming. Brilliana
Tries to soothe them, but on the crest of the wave she's no calmer
Than they, they can tell. Gervase steers. Regal, beside him, sits the Hind.

They're travelling faster than they have ever feared or dreamed.
As they ride, swept aside southerly, the swallowing wave seems
Less terrifying. Already they're finding they don't really mind.

Just Kate lying in the bottom of the boat is a worry
Her eyes are closed. She is talking to herself in a hurry.
With his eyes on Burnham being drowned, Gervase hears her gibberish.

One hand on the tiller he reaches down to caress her brow,
To try to soothe her. She screams for her mam, starting to fit now.
Brilly leaves the bow, holds her. Sophie smiles, knows we get what we wish,

75.

While Brilly's twin, Isabel, holds her tight as the skiff surfs on
Over Burnham into the Levels. The children's emotions
Are still somehow contained and feel safe in the boat; except for Kate's.

Hers are churning like the water below as it gets less deep.
Crashing on trees, hedges, hovels, homes and shacks, cows, pigs and sheep,
The skiff is now being bang-bashed about as it's borne to Westhay

Where finally it stops, midst birches and reeds, as the sun sets.
Darkness, deep as the death of memory, drops like a blanket.
Huddle-cuddling 'neath Paul's winding sheets, the bairns settle, try to sleep.

Only Kate's awake an hour later, but she's still gaga:
Night-daydreaming Paul's alive and full of joy, hope and laughter,
Telling her the war on war's won and wonderful stars will shoot-streak

Across the night sky, each one will be everyone's mam or dad
Forever in joy in life and love and play, and all things bad
Are a concept, like the Lennonian notion of God – for pain

Measurement only; while the stars make sure we're all cared for. Doves
Will fly to all corners of the world and proclaim Care and Love
Have snuck out from under cynicism and ridicule's dark stain.

76.

And, as she said before the wave struck and lifted them up, all
Will be well. 'That can't really be. How can it possibly, Paul?'
She says, writhing and fitting midst the sleepers on the skiff's boards.

'Myself I spoke false. I spoke in hope, which led to you dying.
I cannot cope with that. I don't think I'll ever stop crying.
But only for the loss of you. I'd go too if I had a sword

To plunge in my breast. Without me the these little ones would best find
Sanctuary; somewhere they can be looked after by someone kind–'
'WAKE UP! WAKE UP! You'll help no-one, insane on this boat's floor. Wake up!'

It's the Lazarus boy, Gervase, hold-shaking her till she does.
She wakes to see his angry face looking down at her. 'You must
Not disturb the others. The moon is full and this skiff is jam-stuck

In coppiced blackthorn. Let you and I get out and have a walk,
See where we are, look around, your mind can settle while we talk.
Then we can climb back in and you can sleep more deeply until morn.'

The white hind gets up now and springs over the side on to land.
Her leap seems to switch Katie out of her shaking-fit state and
Time saltates back-forth to sixteen forty two, the year her heart's torn

Engenderings

77.

In pieces by the truth of being orphaned. Her sister's still
In Isabel's arms and both are sleeping. Now she thinks she will
Join the hind and the Laz-boy in this strange, unknown, moon-lit country,

Find her way back to the reality she has to deal with
In the here and now. And despair's timeless, you can't ever sieve
The pain away. Not now and not then, nor any time. Some see

That's part of the human condition, the way things have to be,
But most of us try not to; like Kate now, who can hardly see
Wood for the trees as a ghostly barn owl hoots and swoops whitely

Across the dark blue, silvered night. She tries to laugh, all debonair
But Gervase isn't having it, whispers, 'Hush, you'll wake the bairns.'
She clambers out of the skiff, shamed about what she's not sure rightly,

And hangs on the hind's antlers as her ankles, then knees, squish-sink
Through iced-froze bog. Her feet panic-find a grass tuft. She can't think
Where they might be, sensing only marsh and coldest water. The moon

Then lights up silhouettes of bushes whose branches hold chairs, socks,
Cooking pans and skirts, cushions, trousers, spades, jerkins, bonnets, pots
And the bodies of the drowned starting to rot 'midst beds, crocks and spoons.

78.

Mirrored moons gleam multiply in sedge-surrounded ponds, Kate sees.
Fractured slivers 'twixt silver birches and other marshland trees,
Dire-detritused with decades of domestic human endeavour.

And bodies. The wave's random destructive power's stabbed her heart;
And picking a broken lantern from a branch she wants to start
To tidy everything up, make it right. She stone-says, 'whatever

The day brings, no bairn must see this,' and points at a dead lady
Draped over a bush; 'or that,' looking at a tiny baby
Still-floating, face down. Gervase nods assent, but says, 'Nor pigs flying.'

The moon is so full and bright everything is laid out ghast-clear.
They're on some kind of moor which was wet before but now truth sears
Their vision with fact: angled waters are all around them. 'Dying

Is what we'll all do one day, but not now. Why should we all drown,
When we've got here on a boat?' Kate's matter-of-fact. Her serge gown
Is soaked to the knees. She reaches down, lifts it up to squeeze it dry.

'You're right,' Gervase replies. 'Maybe we can use some of this stuff.'
He slides a bangle from a twig onto the hind's antlers. 'Much
Of it we need.' He looks at clothes and blankets strewn around and sighs.

79.

'We have to keep warm and the winding sheets are just not enough
But how can we cross these wide trenches of water? 'Twould be rough
Indeed to fall in, we would surely die of cold. My feet are froze.'

'Mine too,' she replies, 'We've got to find a way to all keep warm
Else we die. Come, let's get back in the boat, stay huddled. No storm
Will come tonight, all is calm and clear, but I cannot feel my toes.'

They clamber back in and snuggle down with the other children
Under the winding sheets. Kate's grateful for the Laz-boy's will then
To have woken her from her raving and clings to him for some heat.

Outside the hind steps o'er dark black peat diggings and hooks wet clothes
With her antlers from the bushes. She treads carefully, seems to know
Where to plant her hooves, returns to the skiff and lays them in a heap

In the stern. Around her the bog water is now opaque, white,
As she sets out again for coverlets and cloths. Herself light
As the moon, the spectral quality of the night's stiller than still

Except for the tinkle of the baubles dangling on her antlers,
Sedge clit-clattering, and the crackle of ice. Without rancour,
She patiently accumulates what they need to stave off Death's chill.

80.

As dawn breaks the children stir beneath the winding sheets. Kate wakes
First, alert to what she must do to stop them seeing the shapes
Of the victims of the wave outside; thinks razor shells will do well.

She starts sawing strips from the sheet above her, says little ones
Must not see terrible things or their minds threads will be undone
By the desolation of the world outside. She's right, they can tell,

And they all let Gervase wrap blindfolds round their heads with the strips
Kate's cutting with his sharp-edged razor shells. After that they rip
Away the winding sheets to a beautiful gold October day.

Beside them the doe placid-chews grass, decorations rocking
In her antlers, which reflect the morning sun. It's too shocking
To look at the death and destruction everywhere, Kate wants to say,

But the sorrowful mess beneath the bright blue sky fascinates,
And she gawps at the tidal wave's aftermath. 'Look,' says Gervase
Pointing at the piles of clothes and blankets at the back of the boat.

'The white hind must have got them,' he says. 'picked with ease
From bushes the wave's decorated like macabre Christmas trees.'
He gets out, sees the skiff's bow's punctured by blackthorn. 'She can't refloat.'

81.

'Then we will walk! The hind can lead us from this ice-marshy place.
I mean she got these blankets – she must be able to find a way!
Come on, children, keep your blindfolds on and we'll help you from the skiff!'

Gervase wants to argue, say it's too dangerous to keep them masked,
But her spruce pine darkness deep-frightens him, he can only ask
If she's sure. She looks at him like he's an idiot. 'Sure? As if!'

She takes little Sophie from Isabel whom Gervase helps out,
Makes sure she stands close to him then assists her sister. 'About
Just enough room for each one of us if we stay close together.'

He puts Brilly's hand in Izzy's, reaches out for the next child
Who shuffles along the boat's bench, blind-reaching for him in wild
Fear of being left. He lifts the boy out. 'You're light as a feather,

Lad! Here, hold Izzy's other hand.' In this way they all alight,
One by one, eyes still wrapped, and standing in the morning sunlight
Precarious-poised on tufts of frosted grass in frozen water.

'I'm going to wrap each of you in a blanket the hind brought.
'Twill be damp, heavy and cold at first, but they'll dry as we walk
And your parents would rightly be proud of their brave sons and daughters!

82.

Gervase would call this stupid, but deep-knows to follow the doe.
He puts the hand of each child on another's shoulder to go
After her in a line away from this sad site of death and fear.

Kate's at the back. 'Don't peep,' she warns, astonished at how their feet
Follow the hind along hidden dry land. She knows it is peat
Bog they're walking on and what it's for. People must live around here.

Why can she see no plumes of smoke rising into the clear blue air?
Were they all drowned? But the wave surely didn't reach beyond back there
Where the skiff is. Has there been plague or war? Have the people here died?

'You can unwind your masks now,' she calls. We've left the skiff behind.'
'Keep holding onto each other. The path through these ponds the hind
Is finding, is the only way we have. So trust her. Do not cry

Or be afraid. We'll look after you. We have to find some food.
The last blackberries and apples of the autumn are all good
But we need more if we're not to starve. So let's all follow the hind.'

Care-stepping after the deer, trying to leave these huge iced ponds
So that the skiff and the dead can all be become history, gone,
The orphans feel grateful and lucky that their green lady's so kind.

83.

The sun is high now. Another beautiful blue sunny day.
The bairns find apples as they walk and start singing a wassail
As Katie gentle-goads them to follow the white, slender-necked doe.

Then, above the shrill cheer of their apple song they hear a roar
So loud, rough and course, all of them are frozen to the spot, sore
Afraid that some saturnine monster lurks who treats children as foes.

Gervase turns, worrying about Kate, looks her straight in the eye
Sees she's not frightened at all, smiles at that, tells the bairns not to cry,
Says, 'Kate knows all will be well.' Kate smiles back, but then the roar returns,

Loud-closer. The children scream as the hind leaps, runs like the wind
Back from whence they came, leaves them as they are, abandoned, no kin,
Dashes away in huge leaps across the flat ponds, only concerned

To escape from the big-shouldered, thick-necked stag who bellows
Like thunder his possession of the land and females here; knows
That they are his and he is theirs and will brook no interlopers.

His rutting roar reverberates in echoes o'er the Levels.
The Hind can't get far enough away, fearing his terrible
Sexual aggression – he'd as well lock horns as coop and poke her

84.

'Cos her head has branches too, though they're silvered, dressed with ring,
Bracelet, twiggy doll, toy lantern, chain and a seahorse too. These things
Mean nothing to the Great Rutter who wants only to fuck or fight.

She can hear his roar again; he has musk-sensed her need for flight.
Even though she is now lying low behind sedge, full of fright
And panting with anxiety he'll come and find her, use his might

To do what he wants. For neither locking horns nor intercourse
Holds interest for her at all. She simply will not be forced
Into any position which she has not chosen for herself.

She'll neither be herded nor will she use her antlers for war
With him. She'll stay hidden here amidst the dead and their things, sure
That being one of his does or rivals will be bad for her health,

For she is neither. She is what she is, just a brown-eyed, white doe
Not a stag; and, 'tis true, she could respond to a buck's call, though
This one's far too raucous. She sure-does not want to be gored or raped.

And hides in Sedge on a grass tussock, behind fern and thistle
Hoping the flock of long tailed tits with their ticking and whistles
Will distract him. Her task's to look after the children, ease their fate.

85.

But she can't do that cowering here; she has to be wary
When what makes her who she is, makes others treat her as scary,
Confusing, or ridiculous, something 'in-between', easy meat –

'Wanting only one thing', if male, 'asking for it', if female;
These stereotypes sometimes less of a prison than the jail
Of not conforming to either of them, where it is hard to keep

On caring for herself. And so she cares for others instead,
Spends a lot of time, when not doing so, wishing she was dead
For the pain of not being able to belong in a gender.

So hiding here in this marsh, where dead bodies and possessions
Swept here by yesterday's quake-born wave do nothing to lessen
Her sense of being an outsider, requires no surrender

To conformity. Neither fight nor flight. Not really. She'll sleep
Awhile in the morning sun until the old stag decides to keep
An eye on his herd again. It won't take long. She'll dream of difference:

Of seven million starlings flocking in twisting inversions
Of their theme of oneness, corkscrewing through as many versions
Of their smoky silhouette of themselves as their numbers are dense.

86.

The white hind turns pink all over with shame hidden in the grass.
She wishes she could be the same as other hinds and stags, pass
At least for being one. Or the other. Instead she dreams of birds,

An embarrassing androgyne with some confusing issues
Of Self which engender her old, deep sadness she could not choose
Not to live where the sameness lies between the sexes.'Twas absurd

That she played the great stag of Corse Lawn, though the herd was grateful
Somehow, had all been safe, at least felt they were, until that fateful
Massacre a few days ago. The shame of that's unbearable.

Enough to make her want to wade out to sea and drown. And that dream
Is the one she wakes from when she hears the bairns' faraway scream
More distinctly than the stag's roar. And for them she's not scareable –

It's her job to care for them! She rises, feeling new-hearted,
Vows that she will not again let fear cause her to be parted
From them and with all speed ignores the stag and hastens towards them.

She runs faster for fear for them than for fear of the big buck
Who gives chase, but she easily shows him her heels and he's stuck
Ere long. Arriving where their cries came from, she looks, but can't find them.

87.

They're gone! The dell where she left them is vacant. Kate's mam's nightgown
Lying stained, soiled, and crumpled beneath a bush is all there is now.
Antlers glinting in the sun, she scent-senses where they might have fled;

Stares with frightened eyes, twitching ears. The scent of human faeces
And snuffling infant noises prompt her to peer into the trees.
And there, posted in the branch of an oak is Sophie who's not dead!

The belching cough of the stag is not far off. She must be quick –
First hooks antler to gown then nudges the baby into it.
This makes poor Sophie cry so piteously it would break your heart.

And truth to tell the sound of her distress leaves the hind aghast.
She rears in fright. Then the baby turns o'er in her sling at last,
Stops crying as the hind's rhythmic walking rocks her, makes stress depart.

The stag's roar's now further off. He's scared perhaps by baby's noise.
The hind's more frightened Sophie will spill out reaching for the toy
Twig doll above her. How to care for a baby who seems quite ill?

That is the question when you're a deer and the others have gone.
She must find them. Yes. But first she must feed her. She looks so wan
Rejects the doll, instead she sticks her fingers in the hind's nostrils.

88.

Kneeling on a hummock, the hind soft-rolls Sophie out again.
Who inevitably resumes crying. But this ceases when
The hind settles herself round her and offers her warmth and milk.

The stillness of the day and the autumn sunshine induce both
To nap. Then, with Sophie re-slung, the hind rises from her sloth,
Sets off east towards Meare, hopes, if he's here, the stag won't want to tilt.

But how do you care for a baby? What do you actually do?
That gentle widgeon, that know-it-all teal, even that cuckoo
Who should be in Afriki, all know, but not she; not she alone.

Passing another wet field of reeds she sees an old bog hen
Who stand's vegetable-still trying bittern-hard to pretend
She's not there. As a fellow solitary the hind must not moan,

But needs advice, asks the hen how she'd care for a human child
Not five months old, if she were hers. The hen preens, says she'd go wild
With the pride and pleasure of it, feed her the best minnows and frogs.

The hind thanks her politely, urgent-walks on through golden ferns,
Tries again to sense where Kate and the children may be and yearns
To be rejoined with them. To sense where they are, she stands on a log.

89.

And sees with her far-sight the land rise in a high, towered mound,
Thinks in fear of another wave all would rush for higher ground.
She springs back down, will look for them there. And disturbs a red vixen

With war-gold eyes. So she asks her how she'd care for a baby.
The vixen replies she should give her to her; as a lady,
She'll show her exactly how; any problems she'll surely fix them

With the sharpest of clean bites to the throat. The hind's horrified.
She moves smartly away. She just cannot let the baby die.
It would be the final straw in the sorry stack of her failure

To protect cervids first and then children. She would set alight
That stack and make of it her own pyre if she fails to fight
Successfully for the life of this child. Her heart would wail pure

Regret were that to happen now. Meanwhile she must find the bairns;
She'll ask if they've been seen when seeking advice on how to care
For this one. Comes another stretch of water she asks an otter.

'Keep her holted and feed her fish. Chew them up a bit first though,'
The otter says from the hole in the bole of an old willow.
'But six bairns? Sorry, No. Of fish, rats, voles only, I'm a spotter.'

90.

With heavy heart the hind moves on, baby swaying 'neath her throat.
They may have been kidnapped or killed. Their screams did surely connote
Something terrible happened. She will carry Sophie to that Tor,

Hope that there she'll find someone who might care for her, if not Kate;
But the danger in these times of human famine is the fate
All motherless babies have to face: death – life's immutable law.

And that the hind won't allow. Not until her own death is done.
Her sense of the lost children is they've become imprisoned ones.
She'll home in on them with her cervid-certain sensitivity,

Do whatever she can to liberate them. Now feel her zeal
To reparate for the loss of the herd. Let it not conceal
The fact that she is full-ware of the magic of river and sea

Merging with all the world's water and deluging us with dreams.
Her nightmare, as she runs, is the children locked in silent screams
Suffering punishment without walls for their crime of innocence.

She is so troubled by this vision that she trips on bramble.
The baby goes flying as she takes a tumble. Her gamble's
Over, one leg's nigh-broken, limp. Little Sophie's cries are intense.

91.

She's fallen in a clump of golden ferns. It looks like she's on fire –
The afternoon sun's rays halo her in the clear air. They're mired
Is the truth. Hobbling and lame, the hind sad-settles down beside her

To wait for whatever will be. She hears the stag, far away,
Herding does. Sophie's not hurt and fast-falls asleep which allays
Her fears a little, but she must hope no hunters come and find her.

She lays her head on her shoulder, sleeps, dreaming of a baby
With nature's power and the knowledge of an adult lady.
When she wakes up she can see the dream baby's face had had Sophie's.

But in the dream the baby had been able to walk and talk,
Could create famine or plenty, could soften granite, harden chalk
Could conjure storms, melt ice, and suck the oceans dry, make them ghostly;

Could sing soaring like all the choirs in all the world all at once
Yet be silent as the shock when good Archbishop Laud said, 'cunts';
Could be both sides of the war and all the peace at the one same time;

Could truth-be all things and nothing in all periods and places
The light in everything and everyone's many different faces,
The dark space between the diamonds in the universal mine.

92.

Knowing no-one else's dreams, the hind can't find her own too strange;
But looking down at this baby she has to carefully re-arrange
Her preconceptions about infants – Christians have an infant god,

She knows, and her animal brain's just dreamed one too: a mere girl
Of an infant god, it is true, but as her powers unfurled
In the dream, 'twas clear in Jesus's company she'd not be odd.

The hind shakes her head slowly, blinks, tries to wish the dream away;
Looks down at Sophie sleeping, small, dirty, scratched; thinks she could not pray
To that! Then why dream her powerful as weather and strong as earth?

It's beyond her understanding. But she will keep her alive
While her leg will let her, and while she still lives; will help her thrive.
Let hurricane rage and earth quake, of her help there will be no dearth!

The infant opens her eyes, need-looks at her, sees she's not Kate,
Opens her mouth and howls again, loud as all wars. All hell's gates
Could have opened, such is the sound Sophie makes of being distraught.

Which is all very well, but having gone to ground like a fox
The hind needs no deer hunters to find them nor any further shocks.
She has had quite enough, fear-needs quiet, but, sadly, can say naught.

93.

Sophie's screams make her cringe with anxiety. Tiny, they're not.
She's a little baby with big lungs and a temper so hot
There's nothing the hind can do to stop or soothe her beyond singing.

So she sings the quiet song of the deer of Corse Lawn gladly.
A kind mist soft-comes down, but her sprained left foreleg hurts badly.
Still, the baby's found comfort in her warmth again. Her smile's twinkling

Now at the end of her song. The hind sighs with relief. Not so,
Sophie's sister, whose green ear could hear her from afar, got so
Near, homing in on her cries, but now with her silence feels stone deaf.

Dusk's coming down again and the starlings murmurate once more,
Twisting in huge invert-knots like marsh smoke to roost on this moor.
Kate is in despair. Her sister's not crying; the hind seems to have left.

And she? She's circum-creeping like bindweed across the Levels
She knows not where. And the guilt she's feeling she wants to bevel
With that of the hind who has her sister. The other bairns are chained

In a field at the end of Benedict street. They're manacled
To whipping posts. Where their wrists are too small, their tethered ankles
Make sure they can't escape. Being orphaned's the crime for which they're blamed.

94.

On the gentle Isle of Avalon? Yes. Word's come from the East:
Beldams, orphaned children, are apostate; less respect than beasts
Must they be given. Parentlessness is a sin, stenched most foully.

Like whore-crones, who at the least are placed on ducking stools to pay
For their crimes, poor orphans – it is predestined – must not gainsay
The one true Bible's word of God by engaging in popery

And lies. We more fortunate can feel sorry for them, but hell
Is their destination. You can not buy or barter or sell
The will of God. This will the children learn, pinned facing the abbey.

As evidence of spiritual hubris, nothing compares
With its broken roofless walls and tainted chapter house. All who stare
At its desolation, even bairns, can see what makes God happy.

These are the thoughts of the pious Baptist, 'Pure' John Apney, scourge
Of sinners, fast friend of the Witchfinder General who'd purge
The evil from children like these. It's plain from his pamphlet he's just.

John's unsurprised the green one's escaped, but will ensure the rest
Scream the night away staring at the abbey. They can't contest
God's decree that salvation will never be theirs and die they must.

95.

'Let them go, honest John.' It is a pale woman who beg-speaks.
His sister-in-law, whose family name has the Romish reek
Of False Belief. 'Go home to your husband, Anne, lest he beats you sore.'

He threat-shape's with his body: '(lest I do!).' But a godly man
Must, like a New Model Army soldier, show how well he can
Comport himself. 'The souls of these poor children are lost, I am sure.

And by chaining them here to stare through the missing abbey roof
They can watch the sick moon weeping for them and for the sad truth
That though they will die, they're doomed never to look on the face of God.'

He sounds smug, confident in the certain truth-speak of his words.
Checking their chains and knots he tries hard not to feel absurd
After all, he's doing the work of the Lord and that's not so odd.

But he is talking to himself, for the bairns are too little
To understand and Anne's gone. So his certainty is brittle
And as the smallest child cries he wants to kick her, but prays instead

That unlike them his own soul will be saved, he'll get to heaven.
The truth is he's not sure. He turns for home as hope leavens
His fear of death or eternal torment, but leaves the bairns some bread.

96.

Just in case he's wrong. Now, as he comes to the door of his wood-home
His legs won't let him go in. Those poor little bairns cold and alone
And doomed, still trouble him. Not in some sick Catholic conscience way,

But in the way of common humanity. What's right's not right.
He cannot leave them there to suffer. In the one true God's sight
It might be best to put them out of their misery and then pray.

If Herod found killing innocents easy, it's hard for him.
He can not let them die of cold as Hopkins would. It's a sin
To kill them, yet, as well, to let them grow up into sybarites.

For surely, as orphans, that is what they'll do. And sodomites
And Pederasts too. Allowed to mature, it is certain they might
Perpetrate more evil in this world. As certain as this moonlight.

But he can't do what he knows he should and turns back to free them,
Knowing now that like these bairns he's predestined to go see them
In hell. He hunches his back, involuntarily thinking of Abraham.

But he was saved at the last moment from having to kill his son
He wasn't damned if he did and damned if he didn't. At one
With these orphans heading for perdition, he thinks 'I'm bound, I am,

97.

Doubly: I've no choice but to do what's wrong; yet I have freewill.'
This conundrum makes, John Apney's heart race. He cannot feel still;
He can't murder them and now regrets taking them, will let them go.

So he returns to the whipping posts and stocks. They're all awake.
'Please, sir, my name is Brilliana. Please loose me from this stake
And let me loose these others too or we will all soon die of cold.'

She looks blue in the moonlight. 'I put you here for your own good,
Finding you out wandering in the Marshes. I felt I should
Have killed you, but that was before I found out that I am like you,

Destined for hell fire.' He groans, takes his key to her manacles.
Anne comes back with a broth pail for the bairns. John raised her hackles
With his cruelty, but now she smiles, says 'I'm glad not to fight you

Over these poor lambs. Let them shelter tonight in the old pig sty
Where Seth now keeps the winter straw and in the morning we'll try
To see what we can do for them. Come along with me, my dears.'

Over her shoulder she has a coarse rug for to keep them warm,
But on hearing about the sty, Brilly has a mental storm –
Remembers Mrs Raseil. 'Run, bairns! Back to Kate and the deer!'

98.

But they don't. They're tired and cold and would not know which way to go.
And Anne Apney's mushroom-chestnut broth's steaming. She says, 'No!
We'll do you no harm, little ones. Stay tonight. Leave tomorrow

When the sun's up.' Then John says, 'the famine clamp-grips us all.
But Anne is right, this night you should and can safe-sleep under straw.'
Mrs Apney's rug and soup are given in pity and sorrow.

She can see they're famished and frightened, orphaned, homeless and lost,
But she wants to hurry indoors for tonight the dead are tossed
From the Tor, Anwyn, Hill of Souls, to be sent to heaven or hell.

She doesn't want to be out any longer than she need be
When this year's dead souls take flight. She shows them the sty, makes to leave
Saying, 'Good night! John didn't realise what he did. Stay here. Sleep well!'

For all the dead inside the Tor, St Michaels Chapel's like a door –
Opens, frees them from the floor of this world up to the next, sure
For all eternity of their lives consequences, good or ill.

And if you've the ears to hear shrieks of the damned sound more like moans
And the whoops of the saved sound slightly glib like they'd always known
What their fate would be, you might cry that God must toy with us and kill.

99.

Everyone, as part of the human condition, has to die.
Gervase, having been brought back from death, slips outside again, sighs,
Feeling sad, almost missing joining with the souls flight from Anwyn

It's not that he wants to die again, he's just not sure he can,
And he wants to be human: grow up, grow old, die – be a man.
Anne Apney didn't tell him of the Tor, but with the dead he's kin

Anyway, senses all the souls streaming up out into the void.
He doesn't notice, standing outside, how cold he is, feels joy
He does not understand to be out here now on this of all nights,

But doesn't know why; feels star-distant from the children sleeping
Inside the straw store, but close as breath to all the souls leaping
Into the unknown which he only 'sees' with his strange feeling-sight

Does not actually know he senses this exodus of souls, knows
Only a deep longing to merge with the infinite that grows
With how much he is missing the weird white hind and the green girl.

The hind it was who brought him back from death. But she never said,
Of course, why. So he stares, unseeing, as the souls of the dead
Flow up from Anwyn, feeling a dread of understanding unfurl.

100.

He decides tomorrow, together with the bairns, he'll go back
To Avalon Marsh, seek the living plant-girl and the hind, track
Them till he finds them, then go with them wherever they will journey.

He turns, bends and goes back into the converted, straw-filled sty.
Settles down away from the rest and lets his mind gently ride
Where it will and finds himself dreaming of a magic burning tree.

Now you may think phosphenes are just illusory spots of light
Or believe in dread Willow the Wisps and would cower in fright,
But their guilt does connect them: pale fire globes pulse across the stillness,

Stretch over the marsh in a sad fractal line all aglow,
From the hind to Katie Beale. And both intuitively know
Their crime of not caring for their kin connects them like an illness.

So Kate does not need the Sweet Way through the gloom to her sister.
She wisp-walks the wet marsh to Sophie and the hind, must kiss her,
Must kiss them both, glad they're still alive. So, their wisps meet, coalesce,

Become one large, lambent orb around them which humans can't see.
Its radiance shines inwards. Its surface reflectivity
Renders them invisible. They are free to cuddle and caress.

101.

The infant god is incurious, looks through her limpid eyes
At the white hind and the green girl. Does she perhaps recognise
All is certain here on the marsh with freaks of nature; all is safe?

No. She's taken on a human form to find moral feeling.
Being omnipotent, omniscient and power-dealing
Had its attractions once, but became boring. Being a waif

Will help her to find and understand how emotional sense
Of random and impartial cruelty and distressing events
Makes her own creations grander than she herself will ever be.

So having resiled for a while from her godhead, she ur-needs
To feel what it's like to be a mere girl, and that just cannot be
While beguiled by verdigris smiles from her sister who cleverly

Found the hind just now. She needs to get to Auntie Jane, let her
Look after her, mother her, help her find out if it's better
Not to be divine. The best way to learn it is to be orphaned.

'Cos she has to know. She has to learn why it's finer to die
Having made sense or nonsense of life's tragedies, jokes and lies
Than be deathless, all-powerful, all-knowing, of all things the fund.

102.

'Cos you can't be moral if you're the alpha and omega,
At least only in part. And you can never be too eager
Like you can if your heart has feelings and you really need to care

Like Albion's Parliamentarians and Royalists
All of whom share the belief that to do right they must enlist,
Bite the famine then fight each other to display how much they're aware

That God cannot do it alone, needs the help of right-minded
Believers who know that this world is imperfect and who find
That only commitment to the cause will serve to start to mend it.

They are not to know that they were made to have their causes.
That what those causes are matters not a jot. Joining forces
Won't even change that. They're programmed to espouse belief, defend it

Come what may. Well, the infant god inhabiting Sophie grins,
Doesn't mind one little bit which side eventually wins,
Let them believe they're right, all of them; some of them might be right,

They're right, but from her Creatrix perspective it's quite hard to care.
Hence this infantilisation. Through dependency she'll stare
At her carers and learn what this thing called love is, however slight.

103.

Outside, morning's grey, sleeting. The bairns, afar, are warm and snug,
Could sleep forever 'neath the gold-brown hay on Anne Apney's rug.
Dust and dirt are making their nostrils black, but it feels like heaven.

Outside, winter's waking, dank-wetting everything with coldest rain.
Some drips down Gervase's neck. He stares blankly at his mind's chains.
Wrapped up in wanting to be dead again, long-locked in and leaden

As he listens to their snores beside him; remembers merging
With the light of all the stars, becoming all their rays surging
Everywhere across creation. He feels like nothing now at all,

All because the hind just drew him back into being alive
As if he'd wanted to return. But he'd been happy to dive
Headlong into oblivion, had seen everything, heard the call

Of the infinitely small, Wittgenstein's 'whereof we cannot speak'
And whatever the Big Bang happened in. But the hind's strange reach
Has brought him back to this: travelling with orphans, getting nowhere.

His father whom he has rarely met looks at him with contempt
In his mind and his memory. And lying here in this sty doth lend
That glare authenticity. Gervase is not withered by his stare.

104.

It used to hurt, but not now. He'll look after these little ones
And not fear death. He'll embrace it. At twelve he may look half done,
And it's true, in years he is still young; true too: he's back from the dead.

'Come on, bairns,'tis raining without, but we must be on our way
Before that mad man changes his mind once more, tries to do away
With us or makes us disbelieve we'll see our mams again. This shed

We must leave, remembering Katie's promise: 'All will be well.'
The children stir in the straw and yawn. They are warm and hope swells
In their breasts at his words. They smile, longing to see their mams again

'But Gervase,' Brilliana says, 'we don't know which way to go!'
She sits up in the straw. 'Where will you take us? How can we know?
It's cold out there and strange. We'd just be five lost children in the rain,

And now that Kate and Sophie and the hind are gone we're bereft
And scared. There's nowhere to go. We need a home else we'll be left
As food for the crows to pick at ere even a day has gone by.'

'But Brilly,' says her sister, Izzy, 'I'm scared too of that man
Who last night chained us and would have left us to die. We can
Not stay here either!' They look at each other in the gloom, eyes wide.

105.

The cold rain pits the shed roof with a continuous clatter
The children can only shrug, know not what is best. The matter
Is urgent, but they don't know what to do. As a bastard, Gervase

Has long ago accepted that what he has to say's worth nought.
He shifts position to drink the drops dripping from above, his thoughts
And feelings on the short time he was in eternity, amazed

Both that he was and that he's not now; instead he's in a shed
Drinking raindrops with four other helpless bairns wishing he's dead.
The littlest, Jenny, just three years old, cries her need to defecate.

Brilly grins, not knowing what to do, makes a face at her twin.
Gervase tells her, 'Do it here. It won't add to the mess we're in!'
Brilly helps her to the corner, but it is already too late.

'I don't like you,' Brilly tells Gervase, who smiles to hide his shame.
He's always been good at hiding who he is, shrouding the pain
Of fatherlessness with smooth lies and sleek bonhomie. Now he's not,

Flushes in the gloom, feeling embarrassed by a nine year old
But wanting not to retaliate. It's not her fault he's cold
Emotionally. 'I am sorry,' he says, 'I mean that a lot.'

106.

The sound of footsteps slop-trudging purposefully through the mud
Towards their sty silences them. It's Pure John Apney, they judge.
And sure enough, it is he who props open the lid and looks in.

'At the end of days all will be well,' he says under his hood,
Timbre devoid of truth. They nod agreement knowing they should,
For fear of his mood and certainty. But Gervase won't be took in.

'How do you know, John Apney?' he asks. 'Cos it's plainly written,'
John replies. 'In the good book. And as we have all been bitten
By Satan's dogs and will burn in hell, we must do good, act like saints

Now to show the Almighty even the doomed give him respect.
We will travel north east, join Sir Thomas Fairfax, not reject
Jehovah's injunction to preach and fight the ungodly. The taint

Of our sinfulness need not stop us from doing the Lord's will.
So get up and get out of there. Come with me. We can still
Do what is right despite our sins. I have enough water and bread.

We will not starve as we cross Albion to join the Army
Of the Righteous in their red coats. And beware – 't'wont calm me
If you refuse, because it would hurt me to have to kill you dead.'

107.

He does not know he's part Avallach, king of the underworld,
Nor does he know that these two little boys and three little girls
Could help him rediscover his heart and his mind above the earth.

He is so full of revealed ideological zeal that he,
With all true believers on every side, is free, mentally,
To explore, to death, all the caverns and fires below, from birth –

There's always another page of stalactites to God's glory
To be read, more stalagmite truth to be found in the story
Of the need to unify meaning and power externally

By staying underground and idealising the sun
Sky, stars, the origin of life itself in a notioned One
Who knows everything and's imagined to exist eternally.

What John knows is that he is one of Jehovah's soldiers
He will do what is right always and no-one will be bolder
When it comes to fighting the decadent Royalists for God's cause.

'I said, get out of there. Now. Never mind the rain or the cold.
If you die the world will be safer that you didn't grow old.
If you live then your evil serves to test God's immutable laws.'

108.

Whatever he is, Gervase is not stupid and clearly knows
This man is mad. They must do as he says. If his madness grows
They'll be in trouble, but they must all avoid being murdered now.

'Yes, sir, Mr John Apney, and for that we should die. You're right.
But it's better to go with you, try to spread a little light
Before we make our way to perdition, if Jehovah allows.'

He watches Pure John swallow this guff as if it were nectar.
The children follow him out of the shed; now their protector
He discombobulates, as they all stand shivering in the rain.

'Can we take the rug, Mr Apney, to keep us dry a bit?'
Pure John doesn't care. Gervase grabs it from the shed, makes it fit
Around their shoulders as they huddle, feels more hope he might die again

After all, but is sad for Brilly, Izzy, Jenny and Sam
That they will too. They are so cold and frightened, and never can
Last another whole day, trudging up hill and down dale, he would gauge,

But Pure John's now pushing them, telling them to get in his cart.
Gervase is relieved, lifts Jenny up, but she clings on, won't part
From him. 'I'm coming up too,' he tells her. 'We'll have a ride today!'

109.

Pure John cuffs him round the ear for speaking so frivolously.
He nods, helps Brilly and Isabel up. It could prove costly
To say anything. He signals silence, his finger to his lips,

Then passes up the mute boy with no name they have called Sam Calf.
'You'll sit beside me, make yourself useful, clear blocks in our path
Open and close gates; you understand me?' John Apney says and spits.

'Yes, sir, Mr John Apney. That will be all I do: I'll help
You.' Pure John nod's, his mouth grimace is as straight as a shelf.
Gervase knows how to work with rabid dogs like John, secretly smiles.

'This old nag will make good meat one day,' says John cracking his whip.
As the cart starts another slow trip east along ruts and dips
Across what will one day be the bustling high street with cobbled tiles

Of Olde Englande's capital of the commodification
Of mysticism. Beyond irony, justification
Will not be necessary for its peddling of nostalgia

Mixed with spiritual yearning for a magic that never was.
Now as rain vies with sleet Gervase is genuinely awash,
Swim-wet, teeth a-chatter with cold; body seething with neuralgia.

110.

In back under the rug he hears little Jenny whimpering.
'Please sir, we're so cold,' comes Brilliana's voice, try-simpering
To appeal to any kindness John might have. 'Tis right that you should be,'

He growls reply, stares straight ahead through the sideways-slanting rain.
'I will preach to you as we travel, get you accustomed to pain
The eternal reward for your evil – leaving what could have been

(Living safe with your parents) to wander the earth like vermin.
You will be slaughtered; only those left alive will wear ermine
'Cos all God's people must rule and have bright crowns, not just lords and kings.'

The bairns can not listen. In their salv-scavenged Tidal Wave coats
Under their rug they shake, don't hear his words, but the way he boasts
Is colder than death's despair and more frightening than anything

They've ever heard. 'And I'm not talking about actual crowns
Or ermine. You children need to understand and fast get down
On your knees and pray Jehovah will at least, if not you, save others.

We go to join the parliamentary forces, help God's saints
Kill those who would and do wear real fur robes and crowns which taint
England. Their supporters must die too and their sisters and brothers.'

111.

John Apney wants the country to be cleansed, though himself is doomed.
The rain in his face is as nothing now life meaning's resumed.
Nor should it be for sinful children. He turns round, removes Anne's rug,

Throws it aside, tells them they should be glad that the world will end,
Judgement be made. Even though he's bound for hell he will not bend.
Nor must they. Just then, his sister-in-law appears, wants a hug,

'What are you doing here, woman?' he seethe-spits like a spider,
Thin yet fearsome. Gervase looks at him, sees he can't abide her,
'I took the drove, knew you could only take the Wells Road to Hartlake.

I've come with Clubmen, John. It's the only way I could stop you.'
Neighbours then appear from bushes behind. 'We'd rather lock you
Up than hit you, John, but you must let those children go.' Pure John shakes.

His rage is so righteous he would martyr-welcome their blows.
'They are joining God's Saints, Anne! Betrayal's the lowest of the low:
Being my brother's goodly wife does not mean you can thwart God's will.'

His brother, Seth, is among the throng of townsmen bearing clubs.
'We can't hold with Royalists or Parliament people. Our blood
Runs cold as this rain at what both sides will do to ensure they kill.'

112.

To be seen as the same as the ungodly makes Pure John mad.
He slides his long halberd up from the cart and swings it wide, glad
To serve Jehovah despite being called by Lucifer to burn.

His pike's length's more than he realises, his anger stronger.
He decapitates his brother, meaning to, can no longer
Bear any kind of reason, hopes his brother's now in heaven, yearns

That it be so, looking at his poor head lying in the mud,
His eyes reproaching him for wanting to spill even more blood.
Anne Apney's so appalled she's unafraid and walks within his swing

As if he's an insect for swatting. He raises his halberd,
Feels wings rattling, eyes multi-lensing, unbecoming backwards,
Devolving to feed on faeces – a fly. He knows he can do nothing,

He's hypnotised by her holiness, her hurt and his own shame
At having killed Seth and still revelling in it. He can't blame
These friends and neighbours – he's a fratricide, would rather be a fly.

Anne reaches up, takes the halberd from him. Her neighbours and friends
Gather round the cart and help the children down, say, 'that's the end
Of being cold, frightened, we'll look after you. But you, John, must die.'

113.

Gervase will not go with the others back to Glastonbury
Those Clubmen who stay take the rope from the cart, dour, not merry,
But purposive. They loop the rope over an oak branch, sighing,

Not wanting to do this; they've no bloodlust. John's one of their own.
'Sorry John, you have to hang for what you've done. It makes us moan,
So sad to do it,' says one. 'But there'll be no more Apney's dying

With you and Seth gone.' They put Seth's body and head in the cart,
Cover it with Anne's rug. She's gone with the children, wants no part
In this. A grey-bearded clubber soft-tells Gervase he should not look.

Pure John's last words as the rope is put around his neck are mad,
His eyes are popping and he's not even dangling yet. 'I'm bad,
I know, but I've been vouchsafed a vision: over there in a nook

A green girl, a white hind with antlers and a baby have come
To confound my expectations: Hell is indifference! I'm stunned
And I am ready to join them, please let myself and my brother

Join them! Slap the nag. I'm ready to go.' The grey beard tests
The slipknot, nods his head, but Gervase shouts, 'Wait! John could not guess
That what he says is as true here on earth as we've all had mothers!'

114.

They look at him; then they look at John; then look where he's looking:
Limping up the hill a white deer's being dragged by a girl hooking
Her heels into the ground to purchase some pull. The girl's hair's leaf-green.

In the deer's horns a swaddled infant is howling. Even through
This driving rain it's so loud. The Clubmen pick up their clubs. Few
Would ever have believed they would see such a sight. How strange it seems,

Yet ordinary – the girl's struggling and the baby's screaming.
The townsmen put their clubs down again, watch Gervase streaming
Down the hill to join the weird threesome. Their hanging zeal has gone,

But the greybeard rolls up his sleeves and does it anyway,
Drives the cart forth a few paces which leaves John kicking away.
The green girl leaves her deer to Gervase and runs to John. She's strong.

She holds his feet on her shoulders and glares at the assembly
With eyes so jungle-dark, they would feel they're lost in Africki
If it wasn't so gris-cold and wet. They just wanted to do right,

That was all. Why does this teal-green, teak-strong girl arouse their guilt,
They wonder, feeling angry yet sheepish, right yet wrong. 'No stilt
Am I,' the girl says. 'Bring back your cart, old man, so stand he might.'

115.

Kate's amazed he's heard her – Sophie's screams sound echoed in prolonged
Thunder claps as lightning full-flashes in the rain and sleet's Song
Of Winter. Kate's weak now, Gervase sees, reaching them, and relieves her

By helping her shift John Apney's legs back onto the cart, copes
With his weight, holds him, loosens the knot. It's too late. John's neck's broke.
Gervase looks at Kate watching John's head droop. He can not deceive her

And drops John in a heap by his brother. They straighten him out
Together and pull Anne's rug back over both dead men. About
To ask Kate why she wanted to save John, he notices she's thin.

'You need to eat,' he looks at her frankly, 'You're just leaf and twig,
Almost. You'll be under this rug soon if you don't eat!' She's big
With anger then. 'How dare you, you Lazarus boy, even begin

To tell me what I need. You needed me! You've just been rescued.
By me! Now! Let's go back to that town and get the bairns. Let's you
And me put aside our hostility. I beg you, please, Gervase.'

Her whisper's fierce in the driving rain. She's bedraggled, small.
He wants to look after her and shrugs as the sleet comes in squalls.
The baby's cries orchestrate the boom-dreadful din. He's in a daze.

116.

The greybeard Clubman turns the cart around. The others follow
On foot, their collars up, heads bowed, hurrying down the hollow
Back to Benedict street. Gervase, worried, puts his arm around Kate.

'That's Anne's house. I'll take her husband and brother to be laid out,'
Says the admonished greybeard. 'Sophie and the hind!' Gervase shouts,
'Where are they?' Kate's pleased he cares. 'I don't know – maybe a cave? – quite safe!'

They knock on Mrs Apney's door. When it opens, Kate's dizzy,
Not with hunger, cold or the shock of warmth from the hearth, nor Izzy
And Brilly running to greet her, but at the sight of the woman's face

Which could be that of her own mother, Rose Beale, who died at Corse
Three days ago. If Gervase was concerned before, he's now distraught –
For Kate's collapsed and fitting on the porch outside Anne Apney's place.

The twins stop in their tracks. Mrs Apney, tear-streaked, comes to the door
Helps him carry Kate, still now, to the fire, lay her on the floor.
'She looked at me like she'd seen a ghost, yet all I see now is ghosts.'

She asks Brilliana to fetch a cup of warm camomile
And lifting the green girl's head, puts it to her lips with a smile.
Sick Kate believes she sees her mother, feels as safe and warm as toast.

117.

Outside, the thunder's past, but slanting rain wets Anne's fogged windows.
Inside, hours pass, but Kate's ill again, lies like a limp rose.
It's dark, like the place where she'd felt belief before she became green.

She hadn't known Pure John's beliefs, nor that she had tried to hold
Him up when he was hung to keep belief itself alive. Cold
Certainty this is all there is made her viridian hue gleam.

But cold certainty this is all there is, is a brittle truth
Though her greenness gave her meaning – she'd embraced the bairns to soothe
Them, sure her own orphanhood had not killed hope that all could be well:

Perhaps they too could have hope with no belief if she could be good
To them. But so many had died. Perhaps because she was mere wood.
Though there'd been no other way to cope. She had killed them, she could tell,

By neglect. Well, she'd thought, I'll neglect myself too. Now she lies
By Anne Apney's hearth wilting; sees Mam, when she opens her eyes,
Is looking down at her with love, as if all this hadn't occured.

It is all just too much. She is green and Mam's dead, are the facts.
So why is she lying here content with her head on Mam's lap?
'I thought you were dead, Mam, or have my hopes for you at last been heard?

118.

Gervase Cranfield was revived and he's just a silly boy.
But now you too! Or am I dreaming and you're a figment who toys
With me?' Anne Apney shushes her gently, says, 'Just go back to sleep.

When you wake tomorrow all will be different, all will be well.'
Katie smiles and closes her eyes again, but she's shrivelling. 'Tell
Sophie, too, Mam, though I can't hear her cries. This silence is so deep.'

'Sophie?' Anne Apney asks. 'Who is she?' But Katie's re-succumbed
To sleep. Anne looks at Gervase. 'Her sister,' he replies, now numb
With worry for the baby, though he knows the hind's like a mother.

Anne wants to hold the little ones. 'This poor girl is very ill,'
She says, 'which is why she is so confused and so green. But still
If we keep her warm and give her lots to drink she will, I'm sure, recover.'

She carefully gets out from under Kate, gathers the twins and Sam
And Jenny and says she will look after them for as long as she has jam
And bread to feed them with; beyond! She's a widow now, but still strong.

Gervase can see she's mad with grief, but feels she's worthy of trust.
'I'm going out to look for Sophie. She's only a few months old, must
Be cold. They can't have got far, the white hind's injured leg won't last long.'

119.

'You cannot go now,' Anne's anxious. 'Night's drawn in; the rain's not stopped.
It would be folly.' Gervase shrugs, says. 'I must, and won't be blocked.
Kate mentioned a cave where they'd be safe. Do you know of one near here?'

'No. But tomorrow you can take the long drove to Launcherley
To look, or all the way to Wookey if you will. But to see
You'll need the light of day.' She's right, he knows, but must look for the deer.

He promises to come back, is grateful to this kind lady
Then leaves. Out in the rain and dark again he's thinking maybe
He doesn't know which way to go, but will follow his feet anyway;

Just walks, finds he's drawn to a light under the roofless abbey.
Making every rain drop shine like a star. He's relieved, happy –
They're both there beneath the floorless floor, brighter than a summer's day,

Like a picture or a play of Eden before the picking
From the knowledge tree started mean mortality's clock ticking.
He sees he needn't have worried – they're dry, warm, safe and self-contained,

As oblivious to his presence as the town's people are
Of them. Yet aware too. No-one else is here, nor knows that stars
Lodge in the crypt tonight. But the news will bring Kate to life again!

120.

It's as if they're the heart of all stars and Gervase is unsure
His eyesight will survive this brightness, goes round to the side door
And wants to speak, but cannot even look, baby and hind combined

Being more blinding than the sun. He shields his eyes, steps inside.
The hind's leg is not broken or sprained. The baby does not cry.
He wants to tell them about Kate, but perceives they would pay no mind –

They are not of this world right now and it's not clear what they are,
Or even if they are themselves anymore. Colours, shapes and stars
Seem to have fuse-gathered every template and become each other:

Sight is smell, colour is shape, feeling is sensation, taste can hear;
Everything's coming together 'neath this floorless floor. No fear
Doth Gervase feel looking up at the roofless roof as his mother

Joins her mother and all their mothers and all mothers light-streamed
In a merging with their consorts, concerted silent noise beamed
From all the light sources that ever were or will be, just here now.

Gervase smiles as tears run down his cheeks. Since his resurrection
He had felt deprived, cheated. No longer. Now he knows each section
Of everything matters as much, or as little, as he'll allow.

121.

All will be well. He turns away. Sophie and the hind are fine.
He'll go back to the green girl by Anne Apney's hearth. Her time line
On this earth might be short, she looked like a last shrivelled summer leaf

When he left her just now lying by the fire. 'All family,'
Is his one thought walking back to Benedict street. Cannily
He will look after her if she survives, take care of her, feel relief

He's alive at this time in this place to be able to do so.
He knocks on Anne Apney's door. She opens with a smile. He knows
Then Kate must be better. Anne nods, lets him in. He hurries to her hearth.

Kate's eased into ataraxia, lies by the fire. Gervase
Feels relief. Anne points to the bairns in a nook across the way
From her own bed. They smile, then sleep to the beat of Life's caring heart…

Morning breaks. Kate and Anne are talking at the kitchen table
'But you look just like my mam, and sound like her too. You ladle
Broth and bake bread just the way she does – *Mam!?* – How can you not be her?'

Tears leak down her cheeks though there's colour in them now as she speaks.
She looks rosy, like an apple; wants her illusion to keep
Sustaining her. If Anne's Mam, from further searching it will free her.

122.

Sophie's frustrated with this baby-state, is learning nothing
But how dependency means that there is really no bluffing –
You have to be cared for! Her hind-mam's not up to that, not nearly!

'I've fixed her leg, kept us warm and dry last night with god-power,
But it's morning and cometh no woman having come this hour!
It's cheating to intervene divinely too often, but really

This is getting a bit much! I'll have to make my baby cries
Sound a lot louder, that's all!' And she opens her lungs with a sigh,
Goes for quality not volume – whimpering, motherless, parted.

Which, she knows, is a bit rich after last night's show, but she must
Press on with this human need thing to learn why turning to dust
Puts you on the moral high ground. But, not now before she's started

To live even a little. And all that psycho-bio stuff
(That infants' brains develop in bonding with their mams') feels rough
Now she's embodied and having to suffer the consequences

Of having no mother or father amongst her creations.
It is so annoying she could cry. In all ideation
She never envisaged just needing to need without defences.

123.

Back at Anne Apney's house Kate can't accept Anne's not her mother.
Anne says she can't help what she looks like, but she is no other
Than herself. She says she would like to look after them all, but can't;

For now her husband and brother-in-law are dead there's no way
She can produce enough from her hens, and single cow to say
That they will be well fed. 'Four little ones maybe, is all. Your aunt

Will surely have the same problem? Why don't you and Gervase go
To Wells, leave the little one's here. You can fetch them when you know
Your aunt has the room and the wherewithal to look after them. Care

For them as if they were my own, I will till then.' That's a good
Plan, Kate feels. She can go with the Hind and Sophie to Wells, 'twould
Make the trip easier. Gervase agrees. 'Your baby sister is out there,

But don't worry, she's fine. I saw her last night orchestrating
The marriage of heaven and hell, like she was actually making
It all happen, poor little thing, for all time and space everywhere.'

'What do you mean?' Kate asks, angry with him for making Soph sound
Silly. 'I think your baby sister is the infant God, found
In a baby girl!' Kate demurs, 'Nay, 'twas your dreams at which you stared.'

124.

He realises that she has never seen what he saw this last night,
That if she had she'd know he's not deluded at all, just right.
'Kate, your baby sister last night brought the stars down to the Abbey.'

'Is that a fact?' she asks sarcastically, sad he's missed the truth.
Gervase shrugs, knows when the kindest thing is to just extend ruth,
Not try to argue or convince. He knows what he saw, what can be.

But Kate knows 'tis easy to imagine, (Anne still looks like Mam),
And that in this time of famine and warring families they can
Lose sight of what matters – the need to care for others and be kind.

The twins and the toddlers, Jenny and Sam, will be safe with Anne,
She is a warm and lovely lady who despite her grief can
Still find it within her to care for homeless waifs. Her heart's not blind

When it comes to seeing to the needs of others, even when
It's bleeding for the loss of her husband. 'Have some breakfast, then
Leave after. You'll easily get to Wells today if you do not wait.'

Gervase is hungry, but Kate's still struggling to see Anne's not Mam.
She bites once on Anne's bread to please her then drops it from her hand.
Gervase picks it up and gives it back. She gives him a look of hate.

Engenderings

125.

'Your look hates me.' His voice breaks back to a pre-pubertal squeak.
Kate's shocked. 'I just don't need to eat anymore. I don't want to speak
About it anymore either. Don't look at me like that, just stop.'

She sweeps the bread back across the table towards him. Anne sees
What is happening, tells her she must eat if she is to be
Strong enough to face the day; food's scarce, she should eat not to drop.

Kate tries to smile her thanks, but wants to snarl she won't eat again,
Ever. She pulls the corners of her mouth up, tries to make plain
That, as myrtle, she's no need to eat now. 'Thank you, Mrs Apney,'

She says, trying to simper and thinking now she just wants to go.
'I will kiss the little ones a quick farewell and let them know
We'll see them again soon with news, I hope, which will make them happy!'

'Just because you've turned viridian, that does not mean hunger
Can't kill you. I think I had no children when I was younger
Because the famine was so bad. I could not grow them in my womb.

So be careful, young lady, and take food when you can get it!'
Kate smiles; like Mam, Anne won't be diverted. Three knocks. 'I'll bet it's
The minister come to talk about burial, doing it soon.'

126.

Anne Apney's surprised, steps back when she opens the door, full roused
To fear. Strange men with muskets demand to see the man of the house.
She tells them he's dead, but they insist on coming in, making search.

They enter smelling of cold rain and Isiah's god of war,
Their dirty red coats dare anyone not to be very sure
That they are on the side of the Lord of Hosts whose work needs no church.

Satisfied no royalists hide within they begin to leave,
But the last one turns and looking close at Kate says that he perceives
She has the colour of plague, tells her he will pray for her this day.

His words sore-scare her. She does not want to fit or faint again
Had till now believed her transformation was magical – the shame
Of being deemed a victim of plague's compounded by feeling afraid.

From the corner Gervase mutters, 'bollocks.' The parliament man
Looks down at him and spits. Gervase says 'She's green because she can
Look us all in the face and see who we are and what we are like.

She can help us feel the dreams we once had and the ones to come
She is neither a witch nor a saint, just a girl who has won,
At the price of being green, the ability to see us right.'

127.

Though it's not easy being green, the soldier's lost interest
Now in Kate and picks up Gervase by the ear. 'It is best
You come with us, boy, fight the good fight rather than talk the talk.'

'Leave him alone,' Kate cries. Anne says, 'He is sorely needed here.'
But the soldier drums him out into the rain. 'Do not fear,'
He yells. 'He'll be back before Judgement day. In the meantime he'll walk

With friends in the New Model and for his elders learn respect
In the Army of God. 'Twill help him much. He'll learn to reject
The rudeness he's just displayed, and for his evil will be guilt-wracked.'

Kate staggers to the door to see him being frog-marched away
'Midst a mass of red coats dwarf-crowding round him this cold wet day.
She peers after them, memorising their soldierly, god-fearing backs,

Determined that their righteousness will be met by her power
To care about Gervase. She would climb naked up a tower
If she had to, to proclaim love is so much greater than belief

But instead she'll leave the little ones here, follow the redcoats
Wherever they go till she's rescued Gervase; walk, run, swim, float
Whatever she needs to do to keep up with him and give them grief

128.

And so it comes to pass that all those parts of warring England
They'll pass through make alliance to ignore the strange little band
Which will trail the redcoats; like Pure John, if he had lived, would have done.

Full of ironies, life is! The greybeard who had murdered him
Is sad-standing out in the rain wondering how to begin
To make good out of the terrible tale he knows in his soul he's begun

By hanging him. Even though he believed 'twas right at the time,
A sleepless night and a day later he heart-knows he'd lied. Fine
Lines can neither be drawn nor erased from the truth: it had been wrong.

So when he sees the periwinkle girl leave Anne Apney's home,
Face autistically fixed on some task she's set herself, he knows
He just has to help her. She wanders round the town for not very long

Before he beholds the strangest sight a man could ever see:
From the blasted abbey there comes a white deer with a baby
Swaddled like Velasquez's Madonna's child, on its antler's perched

Surrounded by baubles – a twig doll, a ring, a lantern, a chain
They even seem to be dry, impervious to the rain,
As they emerge glis-gleaming from what once was England's biggest church

129.

He watches in awe as deer and baby meet with Kate who hugs
Each one carefully, then gives them milk from one of Anne's jugs
And leads them over to her door. The children all bid her adieu.

He approaches her. 'Young lady, I am an old greybeard, but would
Like to offer you, your deer and your baby, protection should
You allow me. I'm still strong and I sleep little. Needs I have few.

Will you let me accompany you wherever you're going?
I will not let harm be done to you for I must be showing
You and my God and most of all myself, it was wrong to hang John.'

'No, old man, old killer of men. Please leave us be, go away.
You can't be trusted not to do harm, whatever you may say.'
He hangs his head in shame, clearly understanding her truth is strong.

He can not argue with it, knows he belongs with the unclean
And all of those souls who are genuinely not what they seem.
Anne Apney puts a large soft woven purple shawl round Kate's shoulders.

'I hope that will keep you a little bit warm and here is some bread.
It won't last you a day. But I've no more till I bake some,' she says.
I'm sorry you will not stay. Please keep away from any soldiers.'

130.

Kate thanks her, but 'tis precisely after soldiers she's going.
She hugs each child in turn and then shuts the door herself knowing
She'll never see them again, but knowing too they are safe with Anne.

The rain slashes sideways in their faces. Sophie and the hind
Lead the way north and east out of Glastonbury. With no mind
To question the deer, Katie holds onto her neck with her right hand,

Clasps the shawl under her chin with her left, speaks to her sister.
Yet somehow doesn't – 'tis Sophie who 'talks' to her, 'Worminster,
Masbury, then Midsomer Norton, and on; up the Avon is good,

Past Malmesbury, broken abbey'd too, its tiger and flying monk
Mere memories – tourist-packaged as informational junk
In future centuries, and on; towards Milton-under-Wychwood

Where religious pursuit of irony in tasteful saloons
Is borne only by hope-knowing 'tis the end of the world soon,
And on; into the heart of England's families' decline and fall,

And eventually to Naseby we are going. Gervase
Could as well live and die some other time or in different days –
The human condition requires that tragedy must touch us all.'

131.

Kate is quite astonished she's not astonished her sister talked
Without speaking, used words she could have walked
All o'er the world to learn the meaning of and never understood.

Somehow it doesn't matter. They are inviolate, it's true;
The white hind's horns, Sophie's wisdom, her own viridian hue
Are somehow able to spare them from harm. Now she is made of wood

Is maybe why she doesn't feel cold beneath Anne Apney's shawl,
And the lowering skies and sleeting rain do not wet them at all.
It is as if they are from some kind of parallel universe,

Here yet not here for reasons which are certainly beyond her.
'What do you mean, Soph?' she asks, then points straight ahead. 'Look yonder,
I think I see our Mam and Dads.' But the squalls are getting much worse,

She can see she's seen what she wanted to see, what wasn't there
Really. 'I'm sorry, baby, I imagined it. You don't care
Though, do you?' Sophie's eyes say, 'No, but I'm here to find out how to.'

The weather closes in further still. Cloud and rain scuds low and fast
Kate keeps her head down as through the Mendips they serenely pass,
The hind and her sister calm-facing it as if trained by Lao Tzu.

132.

Then she realises it really does not bother her either.
She could be like the old greybeard behind them wearing neither
Clothes nor shoes, just a small black square cloth on his narrow balding head.

His sinewy arms and legs make his hands and feet look big. White
With cold, his once bigger belly, like an upturned new moon, might
Be hungry, but he'll eat leaves, grubs to live to help them be not dead.

The last of the autumn leaves are tossed by winds gust-wild and dire.
The year's end is not far away as they wend into Wiltshire.
The tops of the hills, if they were not so wet, would be snow-sprinkled.

The naked old man following them watches mistletoe grow
Whenever they pause beneath a tree for shelter. It snake-flows
Into airy globes which delight the old man who grows more wrinkles.

His skin becomes more leathery-thick, his eyes more like an owl's,
Following hind, girl and baby, all indifferent to the howls
Of the world around them as they press on purposefully after

The soldiers who took the boy. Villages and Hamlets' shutters
Open as they pass, people come outdoors to gawp and mutter
Prayers and praise. The old man following makes them convulse with laughter.

133.

At Banbury Cross a be-ringed woman, admonished for lewdness,
Wraps a warm sheepskin around the greybeard, meaning no rudeness.
He's glad for it, thanks her for her kindness. 'Kindred spirits, we are.

The natural magic of those three ahead needs caring for.
They're so different I fear they'll be killed by both sides in this war.
I'm here to divert fear and hate to help them on their way, however far.'

He speaks with no ideological indoctrination
Which makes the lady's heart break with wanting to help. 'The nation
Has gone mad with conflicted beliefs,' she says, 'I will come with you.

I'll divert them too with these gold angelus bells between my toes!'
She has a skinny old white horse which she strokes, clearly she knows
And loves her palfrey well, mounts him gently, says, 'just with you I'm true.'

And so they press on through the years avoiding Northampton. Drums
Of war sound from all sides. They arrive at sixteen forty five, some
Three years later at Naseby beating like the heart of all darkness.

Invisible, Sophie and the deer settle 'neath a mistletoed larch
With the white horse. Kate and the adults, though tired from their long march,
Search the red-coat army camp's New Model of disciplined smartness.

134.

As such, a half naked old man and a woman who looks loose
Are tolerated only with religious scoldings: 'Excuse
There's none for being naked, Sirrah, and we want no women here!

In the Royalist camp their strumpets cavort with the devil,
With their long Irish knives and whorish diseases on the hill
Behind the king's men. Unless you repent, there you belong, I fear.'

Thus speak so many of the soldiers who also seem preachers.
Most of them will not harken to Kate's query, want to teach her
Godly ways, or banish her – hell's bane – altogether from their midst.

They reek of right true religion, foul-mingled with stale male sweat.
With their harsh new military methods and stern faces set,
Kate would be scared indeed were she not confident they could assist

Her to find Gervase. She tries to be respectful, polite, but
As the months go by she begins to despair at just how shut
They are to anything save bible study, politics, and war.

Worse treatment is given to the fine lady and the old man.
At least Kate can get moments of their time. She does all she can
To describe Gervase, says he's her brother, will take him home for sure.

135.

If only they'll show her or tell her where he is among them.
But they're keener to ogle and deride her friends as dung, then
Praise the lord or practice their drills. She will take their advice although

She doesn't know that Sophie is orchestrating everything.
She returns to the tree where the hind and Sophie are sitting
With the white horse beneath what looks like all the world's mistletoe

'We've been here half the year and failed to find him. Our greybeard
And fine lady have been abused and the hope in my heart's now seared
By the hot cauterising knife of the truth: Gervase is not here.

Let's go across to the other side and seek him over there.
It's the middle of June and if we don't find him now, I'm scared
We never will, and I must accept it's time to give up, so near

Yet so far from having found him.' The lady and the old man
Join her beneath the Larch where they're all invisible and can
See they must look amongst the Royalists. But as they do, Fairfax

Places his New Model Army of God's Saints atop a hill.
Skippon's in the centre, Cromwell on the right, Ireton left. Still
Unseen, Kate and her friends find a fine way through, and across make tracks.

136.

Down the hill they go; past Royalist troops struggling through wet ground
In order to go up it. They thread their way through and around
These soldiers, who also can't see them, till they reach their baggage train

The hind with Sophie in her antlers has been finding the way
To where the women will be. Only thirteen if he's a day
He surely cannot be with the soldiers, can he? Kate cries again

Secretly, in the same way she has eaten only insects,
And earthworms, stones and soil, fruit and leaves these last six months, and yet
Even as her tears ooze like sap from her eyes she stops them dry

Unsure whether 'tis guilt feelings rather than care for him which
Makes her cry. She wants to go home. Instead, she sees women, rich
And poor in their scared hundreds; camp followers, cooks, washers, whores, wives

In shock as they watch their men fleeing, running back between them
Away. The New Model Army, marching on hunger, can be seen then
Stamping triumphantly on the wounded as they eye the women

In the same way as they look at the Royalist provisions –
As objects to be taken and consumed, (not sexually; God's vision
For them won't allow that, but) by violence with all the trimmings.

137.

Kate can't believe what she's seeing. Sophie just watches, agog
As God's Saints slit the noses or slash the faces of all 'Gog
And Magog's camp-sluts' so they'll ever be branded as prostitutes.

Each and every one, young or old gets her mutilation
Courtesy of the New Model on behalf of the nation's
War against the sinfulness of women. Many die, cut like brutes

They bleed to death, their penalty for being in the female
Half of the human race. Unheard, their piteous shrieks and wails
Can't prevail 'gainst the Eternal Truth guiding the acts of these troops.

How could they? Kate wants to go home, has forgotten that it's gone,
To be in the arms of her mam again. Then she could go on.
But right now feels the sole way to be with Mam is to be dead too.

She wants to walk out amongst these men let them do as they will,
But the hind and the fine lady won't let her. 'You must stay still,'
She says. 'Your task is to help your sister find what it is to feel.'

If Kate was green before she now becomes darker than forests
Of blue-black Norsian pine, spruce-knows she will now never rest
Until or unless she can find a way to make all this unreal.

138.

Mistletoe entwines above them. They remain invisible
Kate wants to go home. The redcoats' deep bloodlust is risible,
But she's not laughing, she feels ashamed to be a human being,

Wants to gather all these women with her here under the tree,
But instead has to close eyes and ears to the savagery
Of the soldiers slicing and slashing, feels vile at what she's seeing,

Not lucky not to be a victim, just guilty she survives
Amidst the perpetration of carnage, shocked and horrified.
It's completely beyond her. She moves her head from side to side

Unable now to cognise properly this atrocity,
How disciplined men treat innocent women with no pity.
She can even see dispassionate glee in their hooded, sour eyes.

The hypocrisy of that is more than she can bear. She winds
Her feelings into more mistletoe, grinds it out, doesn't mind
Concentrating on that, losing consciousness in solely green thoughts.

The blood and bodies of animals, even these human ones
Have always provided the soil with nutrients. Kate is done
With being human, would love to stop caring, but can't. She's too fraught.

139.

She wants to go home and tells herself that's where Gervase will be.
She cannot stand what's happening in this war-hell called Naseby.
Unbearably, it does not stop. She'll take Sophie back to Corse Lawn.

It cannot be hell there too. Not anymore. Everything moves
On. Even gauche poetical sentiments can be shoe'd –
Horned into idiot metre and awkward rhyme, real life shorn

Of reminders of such horrors over centuries of time,
Surely that is how it should be? How else could we ever find
Peace? She nods; yes, the blandishing of history will lighten this load.

To carry it in her memory would make sponge of her brain.
She wants to find a home somewhere; to live, belong and remain
Recollection-free of this and her helplessness along the road

To find poor Gervase, a project at which she's dismally failed.
She'd been so horrid to him back when he'd been slimy as a snail,
But now she feels nothing but remorse for treating him with contempt.

He's resourceful; he'll find a way back from this 'Heritage' site,
If he lives. Surely? Not stay with these troops with their right and might
Religiously perpetrated against women with violence.

140.

When everything's always awful it always plays on one note.
By killing women, cutting cheeks, nostrils, septums, the redcoats
Make worse than bad music. Kate stops up her ears and shuts her eyes

Waiting under the tree with Sophie and the other four, bored
By the stupid banality of horror. She waits years, more,
Forever, for it to stop. She can't get inured, though hard she tries.

Centuries pass. Still the cacophony of conflict prevails.
Kate, the lady, her white horse, the greybeard, and the hind daren't fail
To remain invisible while Sophie feel-observes what war means.

Not by seeing the surge of sensation God's Saints are riding
As they mete what their maker requires, always abiding.
Nor, as Goddess of War, by hearing the clamour and fear she gleans.

Not even by all the death she wreaks, or the pain or the hurt.
It's the *feeling* – the sorrow, grief and caring, that puts them first,
Puts them above her morally. She must learn this thing called caring.

She was right to incarnate. To be nurtured by a mother,
To be cared for, will help her find how she can care for others.
But for that she must be helpless. And for that she needs to have daring.

141.

The daring to die. That is what she has to take on to live.
More than that, the daring to care in the face of death, to give
Of herself knowing there's nothing more important, nothing at all.

It's what love is. Like the mistletoe above them in the tree
Love and care seem to thrive on loss and death, seem on them to feed;
Though this is a hard thought to swallow without feeling confused, small.

Like an infant. Like the infant she is. But the Almighty
Can do as She pleases! And it pleases Sophie to bite the
Hands that have fed her. The hind and her sister, she must be leaving

So that she can do the baby thing in full need-dependence.
It is the only way she will learn the meaning of love and hence
Have parity restored with these emotional human beings.

With her omniscience she full-knows it has to be this way;
That Aunt Jane's died here too, had been forty if she was a day,
Too old to survive her ruptured spleen courtesy of cavalry

Who'd earlier charged down her royalist foot-soldier husband
Who'd volunteered in support of the divine right of kings and
Took Aunt Jane with him, motivated by hunger and heraldry.

142.

So she knows she has to feel, cannot live on omnipotence
And omniscience alone, must now leave all this violence
Give herself as a small baby to this fine lady, Ruth; need her.

Unbeknownst to the woman herself she makes the fine lady
Say, 'Robert and I are lovers now. Let us take your baby
Sister back to Banbury Cross, Kate. We'll love her, clothe her, feed her!'

The greybeard, for it is he who's called Robert, warmly agrees.
'She will be safe with Ruth and I, and happy because, you see
We'll adopt her as our very own and love her perennially.'

It is bizarre that all around soldiers are dispensing death,
Women are being cut and sliced, many breathing their last breath,
And here are these two wanting to keep Sophie permanently

Like they're in some modern council office with social workers
Chatting about her care. They've been so helpful, not shirkers
In the task of helping her look for Gervase, but Kate cannot say

'Yay,' because Sophie's not her daughter. It's so strange being asked
To take responsibility to relinquish it. The task's
Beyond her, so Sophie nods Kate's head, makes her speak, 'I can't say, Nay.'

143.

She shakes her head, makes it her own again. 'I want to go home,'
She says, acid green with the bitterness of that. 'Yes, I'll hone
My sense of direction and if I ever find it, I'll come back

And ask Sophie if she wants to join me there. In the meantime,
Yes, she will be best staying with you both. You have been so kind:
Helped me look for Gervase. Everything I fear's what I am, alack.

I fear being homeless and alone. I'll go back to Corse Lawn.
Gervase, if he lives still, will have done the same thing, I am sure.
An inner voice tells me my aunt's died here too. There is nowhere else

I can go now.' Then Ruth soft-says, 'you can come live with us too.
This must be one of the last battles of the war, I fear you'll
Fall foul of lost soldiers on your own. No? Well, these women are Welsh.

You could walk west with them, I 'spose, those still alive, if you insist
On heading back to where you came from.' Kate understands her gist,
Says, 'People see what they want to see. We'll be alright, Hind and me.

Thank you.' Children cry for mothers. This slaughter will be done soon,
The redcoats are cleaning their knives on their victims' clothes. The moon
Rises balefully, skull-white, as they purloin what they will, well pleased.

144.

Then they leave, sweeping motherless child-stragglers along with them.
And the battlefield becomes a dump: corpses, wailing women,
All the waste of war as mid-summer darkness finally falls.

Holding the white horse's bridle, Robert waits for the lady
To settle herself side-saddle. Kate kisses her small baby
Sister who for a moment seems bigger than the sky and as tall

As history's long passed yet stretches ahead interminably;
Then passes her over, knows she'll not see her actually
Ever again. Sophie leaves her the legacy of time travel.

Foreseeing all, forgetting naught, able to move through time where
She is, if she chooses. She knows not about this now, feels scared.
As she watches them leave beneath the moonlight. Her heart unravels,

Starts pumping green blood beneath her green skin. Transmogrifying,
She feels there's no point not putting down roots. Transmogrifying,
She will walk with the hind to where she can feel she truly belongs.

Somewhere she can feel whatever is around her without fear.
Somewhere under the rainbow where, anonymous, you feel cheered
By your virtual stillness; transmogrifying making you strong.

145.

But what has become of the shy liar Gervase Cranfield?
Having already died once and seen his whole life, like a film, reeled
Out before him, nothing that then happened to him was a surprise.

When the redcoats took him from Glastonbury six months before,
He kept secret, even from himself, that really he was sure
That though, unlike Kate, he could not traverse time, he did have sharp eyes

To see both what would happen and what had happened very well.
The price he paid for this vision was to forget how he fell
Exactly in and out of each event of his subsequent life.

You cannot have everything, of course. He'd laughed himself rotten
When arrested, that he had once known and had now forgotten
What happens next. God's Saints, (the redcoats were so grandiose), felt strife

Worming within them, sensed the boy was lunatical, mystic,
Able to laugh at things they could not see. They beat him with sticks
And chased him off two days later when they'd arrived at Malmesbury.

He'd ran like the wind down the steep-south facing hill, quite certain
Intuitively that he'd be safe. Though rain streamed in curtains,
And he'd felt froze as he flew, he'd been unharmed, could head for Tewkesbury

146.

Living off rats, worms and the kindness of others on the way,
Worried about his former companions, but mostly Kate.
He could not remember from his death time what would happen to her.

All he knew was that 'twas not Wells he should go back to, but Corse
And that he should prepare the earth for a burial. His thoughts
Were grim. Things he 'saw' when his life flashed before him, were now fewer

In his memory. He knew he saw them, but as he trudged
Was irked he'd forgotten what would happen to her. He judged
Himself harshly for letting the redcoats take him too. Poor, small Kate,

So green she was and so thin. She is probably dead by now,
He thinks, passing through fields empty of livestock, hens, pigs, sheep, cows.
So why does he hurry now to get to Corse, fear he'll be too late?

He can only guess she is dying or dead and keep going North.
Through Brokenborough, Little Larkhill, on past Gloucester. He'd taught
Himself to go on. His task is to just go on until thunder,

Lightening, hunger, old age, (he can't remember which), strikes him down.
Through winter sixteen forty three he passes Tewkesbury Town,
Arrives back at Forthhampton, then Corse; curious, full of wonder.

147.

And anxious too, he is too late. Winter springs to wet Summer.
Watery skies pastel perfect rain for marrow and cucumber.
Gervase chooses the heart of the old deer run to dig, turns the earth.

It's flat and grassy here. He comes every day and forks the ground.
Evenings at his mam's hovel by the manor, he can't get round
The fact, despite this preparation, of Kate and the hind there's a dearth.

The green girl and the white hind do not tempt the fates or furies.
They don't hurry, dawdle often in different centuries
As they spend the summer walking due west. Kate's no longer worried

About Gervase, has sensed he still lives long after her final change,
Delights, with the hind, in not being visible as they range
Towards the setting sun's resting place, at peace and in no hurry.

She'll put down roots soon and settle down at last, glad to be still.
But that's when they've got back to Corse Lawn again. For now she will
Enjoy what it means to walk across England's green and pleasant land.

She'll love the Emm One and the Emm Forty, sleeping in Oak Trees,
Watching froglets hop from ditches and tasting wild strawberries,
Admiring Morris dancers, Morris minors, coal men and girl bands.

148.

But eventually, the autumn of sixteen forty three
Calls them both back to Corse Lawn from cruising other centuries.
In a misty late afternoon in October, they're glad they've returned.

Through the trees the six hundred deer hadn't reached a year ago,
They emerge. Kate's heart quickens to see Gervase bending slow
And steady, forking over a patch of meadow earth, rhythm firm,

Absolutely concentrated on his work. She calls his name.
He drops his fork, turns slowly. As if waking from bent-backed shame
He straightens and with a huge smile opens his arms to them both.

The hind trots to him. As she follows her, Kate enjoys moving
Her arms and legs these last few steps, finds it so very soothing
To know walking is over soon. The feeling is not one of sloth.

It's one of love and truth co-mingled. Time, space and shared meaning
Come together in the shy smile she has with Gervase this lovely evening
As he hangs a tiny gold candlestick on the hind's antlers.

'I've come to go,' she says, unable to stop smiling . 'I know,'
He says. 'I'm here to help. I'm happy to see you. Time went slow
All the time we were apart. I'm glad you're here now.' And he thanks her.

149.

As the night falls the moon rises full and bright. The hind too shines,
Adding her light to the scene, shadowing the turned sod. Kate's fine
Features and stick-like shape look lovely to Gervase who's wide awake.

He hardly wants her to step into the shallow hole he's made
For her, but knows that she has to. It is not so much her grave,
As her home. She's not afraid and she smiles because here she'll be safe.

She tells him she searched and searched for him, but truly it was home
They've both been looking for and for her that means being alone
Here for hundreds of years in all weathers, combusting in the dark

Every night when no-one is looking. 'Except for me, please,'
Gervase half-begs, half-states, love-lorn. 'Except for you,' she agrees.
Stepping into his hole. He fills it in. Night and day birds sing. Larks

As well as owls, nightingales and collared doves, warblers, nightjars,
All share the stillness in melodic harmony with the stars.
Her arms and hands and facial features all ur-change, begin to branch.

Taking the ornaments dangling on the hind's anlers, Gervase
Places them carefully on Kate as she twists and turns like a maze
Into a tree. She branches and twigs and leaves. He finds he's entranced.

150.

Then she burns before him, combust-firing flame from every leaf
In a downside-up shower of gold and orange lung-bursting heat.
He has to step back to see and in doing so he sees himself tending

To her every need over the years of the rest of his life.
He sees her embrace sky and be caressed by air and feels like
She sends the army of all emotions back into the ending

Of the world that the ideologues and religious nuts
Are so keen on making. In the crackling of flames she cuts
Through their desecration of the earth and he can hear her laughing

Like she's some kind of sense of humour tree, her tongues are licking
The pomposity of those who think they know that in picking
The beliefs they have that they are right. It's like a bad case of farting

When curtseying to the queen. Because it all doesn't matter,
She knows, we're here to do our best to be kind. Not to flatter
Or hurt others. Just to be kind, maybe even contentiously.

Everything else is just tea-cupped storms, and not to be borne
With any strain. She is happy to delight, as if love-lorn,
In simply being – rooting, branching, twigging conscientiously

151.

By day, leaves green-reverting to their pre-fiery state at dawn,
But conflagrating blindingly by night as her ghost walks, wan
With distress and hope as she seeks out the shell-shocked in every war

That ever was or will be, the raped, the wounded, the bereaved
From the Congo, the Flanders trenches, and the Leningrad siege,
From nameless dead soldiers' families to slaves shipped in confusion, sore

And numb, all of them, lost and abandoned by a world which wreaks
Sorrow and heart-break so blithely it's impossible to speak
Of what you feel or saw. Their minds broken, feelings dissociate,

Split from emotions by bullets, bars, chains, famine, rape and fear
They're like ghosts of war themselves, regardless of where or what year
She finds them in. And it's curious what she does to dissipate

Despair, disperse it all away. Even Francine Shapiro
Would have been proud, if Kate was alive. But as a ghost, near though
She is still to suffering, Kate is dead now whereas these possessed

Are actually still living. She visits them in their place and time
Wherever it is. From Tenochtitlan to Lhasa she finds
The living left behind and with rhythm attends to their distress.

152.

She taps each shoulder or waves her ghostly hand before their eyes.
Split off from feeling, they see, as she moves it from side to side,
That their memories can be moved on, they can come to feel again

Though they cannot see her, don't know she's there helping them let go,
Unblock and open the bridge twixt what they feel and what they know.
They can grief-howl into the ages if it helps them ease their pain,

Guilty they've survived when those they cared for have died and are gone.
She just taps them rhythmically, wand-touching left-right-left-right, on
In sets, a secret witch-ghost for good, as they come to terms with shock

At what's been done to them. Which is where we would leave her: by day
Just a tree; by night burning, as her ghost, whose name's Agape,
Waves away the effects of vicarious violence and stops

It patterning the rest of their lives, if it weren't for the fact
Sophie has caused so many people's minds to break inside, smacked
Silly by their God-bestowed fates which prompts Kate to kind-give mercy

To them with her side-to-side waving. She knows how hurt they feel,
Swaps their pain for her movements, then finds the weight's too great, and kneels
beneath this human sadness world, holds feeling's geo-buoyancy,

153.

As if she's dark matter supporting everything everywhere –
Huge nebulae to tiniest quanta of everyone's cares.
And the cost's negligible – she's already dead. Her ghost can bend

And flex beneath anything in the end, go on forever…
One day in Banbury, she finds a woman unsure whether
To hit her head on the stone wall of her cottage to feel. Kate wends

Her ghostly way over to help, recognises Ruth Greybeard
The fine lady who married mad Robert, made him less weird
With love, then adopted her baby sister, Sophie. As a ghost

Kate can't speak to her, even hug-greet her again, only wave
Away her mental pain, without being seen. But this woman saved
Sophie thousands of shocked souls ago. Longing to see her utmost

On Ruth's mind, Kate's spritely palpitations pulse so rapidly
She follows Ruth from washing line by dry stone wall vapidly
Almost frightened of what she will see. Ruth's white horse neighs in alarm

As Kate hurry-passes right through him after the be-ringed Ruth
Who, unlike her tethered horse, doesn't see or sense her. The truth
Is syphilis is scrambling Ruth's senses. Raped, she's been sore harmed.

154.

Defeated soldiers killed Robert before they did their abuse
Of her. Eyes forced to watch his murder, she could not refuse.
After they got home, Sophie made the best of it, thought Ruth would learn

About human suffering's nobility and love's triumph
Over pain and death and wrap herself in being a mum for
Her, became more devoted to meeting her needs and would not yearn

For Robert, would forget him, find motherhood's its own reward.
But, in fact, Ruth's heart for her seemed to have been put to the sword
And having become human – need-full – Sophie can't change her at all.

She cannot revert to omnipotence, make Ruth's hurt heart feel
Connected with her again. Sophie's frightened at how real
The business of helpless dependency is, worries Ruth will fall

Permanently into this state of mechanical caring
For her which gives her nothing to thrive on, no proper sharing
Of feelings and minds. There is no child-and-mum pleasure she can take

With Ruth so dissociate she cannot even smile. So scared
Does Sophie feel about this she finds herself bawling, aware
Only of her need for mother-love, deep as a bottomless lake.

155.

Down which she feels she's falling, drowning like the heaviest stone.
What price now dependent infancy and the comforts of home?
Daring to love and die holds no attraction now it's not a choice.

With omnipotence gone she feels as if she has no power
Whatsoever. With omniscience diminished there's no hour
Of the day she's not frightened. So seeing Kate's ghost makes her rejoice.

Or does she ludic-imagine she comes to her, bends and smiles?
Sophie wishes she could just speak, tell her everything, but while
She is alive she is sadly subject to humanity's rules

Of development and though babies can make sounds, they can't string
Sentences of words together. She can laugh or cry, but bring
No narrative for her worry that trauma's made of Ruth a fool

Who just stares at her distracted, if she looks at her at all,
Lost in her loss and her shock and disease, ignoring her calls,
Unable to care. 'Katie! Help me. Please!' Sophie wants to implore.

Then she despairs. Kate's ghost-touch has no substance. Even the breath
Of a butterfly would have more impact on her skin. Kate's dead,
Sophie knows her intuition's fooling her. Katie's dead, she's sure.

156.

As she looks down on her little sister, Kate deep-sees their mam
In their shared stare. There! There is Rose Beale. Sophie feels her too, can
Only look vaguely where Kate is with round eyes, deep-needing their mam.

Not the sad face of her adoptive mam, Ruth, who's staring too. Void
Are her eyes. She can't see Kate and just ignores Sophie. She toys
With a thread in her skirt, looks out her back window. The hills she scans,

Nervously, for marauding soldiers. Why they killed Rob and raped
Her, but did not take her white horse, Ruth cannot understand; takes
No comfort from uncertainty or this small other-mam'd baby.

She notices an even paler, parchment-coloured creature
Outside in the paddock, beside her horse. She knows those features!
It's the deer who far-carried Sophie. Does it want her back? Maybe.

It is standing stock-still beside the horse, as if attending
To some scintillating secret and somehow thereby mending
A rent in the fabric of what matters. Ruth shakes her head, feels mad,

Wants to hurt herself to bring herself back into the present
So she can meet Sophie's need for her to be alert, pleasant,
Punctures the back of her hand with a nail though it makes her feel bad.

157.

Her involuntary yelp diverts Kate not from her sister,
Though she's not forgot either she's here to help Ruth resist her
Nightmares and awful memories, render them harmless and banal.

Kate sees Ruth has washed Mam's white nightgown – it's now a bedspread
From under which Sophie lies staring at her, her little head
Still, her eyes fixed wide, following her like a barge up a canal,

As if she sees a ghost. 'I'm a ghost by night, by day a tree.
It's mad what has happened to me. But 'twas Ruth's sadness, Sophie,
That brought me here. She will love you more easily after I'm gone,

I spend all my ghost time being wander-drawn to people shorn
Of happiness and hope by horrors of war. Back to Corse Lawn
I then return each morning, take in daylight again, feeling wan.

But able, as a tree, still to find calm-strength in having leaves
So that I'm ready to wave or tap for the hurt and bereaved
By evening again. Sometimes I simply wail or moan two notes.

It seems to be enough to help them. But I wish I could die
Properly. Our real home lies in not-being. My heart sighs
For that real home, but it seems fate's decreed I must be a ghost.'

158.

Sophie can't see or hear her, knows with intuitive eye-sense
She must fix her gaze there by the window where the daylight bends
Around the vacant, near-dream-unreal half-shape of her sister, Kate.

It moves away toward Ruth in a gentle swirling of motes
Of sunlight-dancing dust. Ruth's eyes dart, as if taking notes
Of all she's been through, from side to side. Maybe it is not too late

For this woman to recover her capacity to care
For her again after all. Sophie gives a little cry, shares
Ruth's terrible memories, gives voice to them in her cuddle-needs.

Ruth ignores her, looks ever more hurriedly from horse to deer
And back again, over and over. Then she returns to here
Now, lets the past go, pours broth for Sophie and sits her on her knee.

Seeing Ruth's recovered her mind, Kate deep-wants to hold Sophie;
But having no substance she can't. And her sister's no trophy
Anyway to lift up in triumph. She looks at them both, feels pleased

Wants to linger here and just watch them do 'mother and daughter'
Together, remember her baby-self with Mam. This thought's her
Envy's comfort as she wends her way like smoke through the walls and leaves.

159.

Outside in the paddock, the ancient white horse swishes his tail
As the hind, who sees her perfectly well, joins Kate. She can't fail
To see too that Kate is crying slow silent tears which don't glisten

'Ruth's rape will kill her before long. Who'll then look after Sophie?
I can't believe that such fates befall small babies. If only
I still lived instead of doing this ghost work. I can't listen

Anymore to other's awful plights, wave their worries away.
I know of no ghosts who remove illnesses or stop death days.
So why should I have to ease shocked minds? Must I go on? If so, why?

The dead should be released, shouldn't they? So why am I made a ghost?
It is a punishment, I think, for what I did wrong. The most
Evil of all the things I did was to cause poor Paul Bier to die.

Perhaps I'm in hell? That's why the nightly flaming of my me-tree
Makes me wander the world for the broken hearts of the pitied.
But I don't care about them, whether they love again and start to feel

Once more. I don't care! I've had enough! I just want to depart,
All this, but don't know how. Show me, dearest friend, where to start.
Please! I can't go on being a comfort to others. It's unreal.'

160.

The hind feels so cross. It's not as if she's of this earth either.
Kate's self-pity as a ghost is ghastly, makes the hind prize her
Cervid status, as her antlers drop off forever, more highly.

It's time to leave time altogether, she thinks, heavy-hearted,
Realising Sophie's power is such they'll never be parted.
Babies are always babies across the species, she thinks wryly.

And regardless of when. Nothing is more important or pure
Than life's need to start small and vulnerable, completely sure
Only that random luck and love can help it develop and thrive.

Roundly radiant with need, all power-mad and all knowing
So that each one has an aura of potential which growing
Will realise. They can't be painted by artists dead or alive,

Their little features fudged roundly as they elicit soft smiles
Of recognition. They carry so much hope while all the while,
Here and now, actually they're helpless, hopeless and wholly 'cute'.

Which is all Sophie is by now, just a baby, the hind thinks.
Now Kate's a ghost she can't see that life's over in an eye's blink.
Love all babies, Kate, becoming out of nothing – god made minute!

161.

Yet Sophie was as truly bored with being God as you are
Being a ghost. I'll take you to Putney where babies are stars.
We'll listen to soldiers argue for ideals and interests

And their words and their passion will inspire centuries of hope.
But our concentration will drift to the mighty Thames which lopes
Like a leviathan as the tide rolls in. And what will be best,

As the night comes in with it, will be all of life's infancy
Ghost-gathered on the bridge of boats for shining necromancy.
And there I'll leave you to lose yourself in becoming a baby too!

As Anwyn was where dead souls rise up, St Mary the Virgin's
Where the waters break and they fall again as babies, urged in
To this world's wombs once more. Destined to take a biased, moral view

If they are human, or just to be vulnerable, dependent
And full of appealingly fluffy potential if they've been sent
In other forms through the myriad birth-canals of creation.

And all as light as and as different as there are stars in the sky.
It would blind the living to see it, but you're a ghost. That's why
You have to go there, become part of the infant congregation.'

162.

The green girl's ghost hears none of this, simply senses with the hind
She must go, leave her flaming tree to stand stark, leafless, behind
As dead wood, then drift like smoke to the east where war-leaders make peace.

So smoke drifts as the wind blows. The Putney she comes to shimmers
And shifts as it swirls, like the waters of the Thames, with glimmers
Of different times and ages. Once, Elizabeth Tudor she sees

Step from a discreetly curtained, gold-leafed lighter. John Lacy,
Her lover, holding her hand o'er his threshold to privacy.
Another time she sees a fire-starter between buses and cars

Running with sirened excitement from the fierceness of his flames.
But sixteen forty seven's at last where time stands still again
For poor Katie's anorexic, insubstantial, green ghost to start

Her final descent into unbecoming and being poured
Into a new life to be reconceived as far from gun and sword.
As the debaters' discussion of property and power

Is from the death by hunger and disease that Brilliana,
Isabel and Sam suffer in Glastonbury, garnered
By Anne Apney's succumbing to dementia's baleful glower.

163.

That is, not very! But the link seems academic merely;
Completely unlike the flight they now take, wanting to really
Take the time twixt the trip to what is next and death's release from pain

To join Kate here in Putney as Cromwell berates confusion,
And Levellers speak for equality. The child-ghosts muse on
How little they understood while alive. Now seeing Kate again

They are easy in themselves, somehow know 'tis best not to mind
They're ghosts because billions of babies, all species and kinds,
Though they are nebulae, each one, are all here on the bridge of boats

Visible to each other and the hind on St Mary's Tower
But to no-one alive. If the Thames waters' churning power
Could speak they would warn you, 'Look away. See only your own eyes' motes.

For if you can see that babies are really what you call god
You might cry yourself away into forever at how odd
And incomprehensible is life's oxymoronic essence.

And if you don't, you will have become as dim as death fighters.
So see only the barges and shallops, long boats and lighters.
Then festinate fast and furious, back to something more pleasant

164.

Elsewhere. Take the 'Agreement of the People's long legacy
Down the revolutionary road to true democracy
In France and America as families fight for hearts and minds,

If you want. But just go! Tell yourself and your loved ones Berkeley's
Tree falling in the middle of a wood, to put it starkly,
Does not exist. And neither now do Kate, Sophie or the hind.

With Brilliana and Izzy, Jenny and Sam they've been re-wombed.
Their great, great grandmothers great, great grandmothers are sweet-attuned
To their needs, have them at their breasts and give them warm love and nurture.

So you need not worry about them at all. The hind's returned
To Corse Lawn to give Gervase back a sense of magic. He'll learn
To smile, find joy again. He's had enough dark thoughts, needs to search the

Secret parts of his heart not to find loss again but wonder
That he once died and went to Putney too, but was not sundered
From his life after all because he's vouchsafed to know finally

Now, in the autumn of humanity, the huge roiling roar
Of the world's sonorously swollen waves drowning every shore,
Can help you feel all will be well. It's how it is and has to be.

Engenderings

www.ingramcontent.com/pod-product-compliance
Lightning Source LLC
Chambersburg PA
CBHW080843270326
41928CB00014B/2882